SOVIET HYPOCRISY AND WESTERN GULLIBILITY

SOVIET HYPOCRISY AND WESTERN GULLIBILITY

SIDNEY HOOK
VLADIMIR BUKOVSKY
PAUL HOLLANDER

PREFACE BY ERNEST W. LEFEVER

ETHICS AND PUBLIC POLICY CENTER

Library of Congress Cataloging-in-Publication Data

Hook, Sidney, 1902-
  Soviet hypocrisy and Western gullibility.

  Bibliography: p.
  Includes index.
  1. Propaganda, Russian—United States. 2. Soviet
Union—Foreign opinion, American. 3. Public opinion—
United States. 4. Communist strategy. 5. Peace.
6. Disarmament. I. Bukovskii, Vladimir Konstantinovich,
1942-   . II. Hollander, Paul, 1932-   . III. Title.
DK279.U6H66 1987   327.1'7   87-3545
ISBN 0-89633-112-1 (alk. paper)
ISBN 0-89633-113-X (pbk. : alk. paper)

Distributed by arrangement with
University Press of America, Inc.
4720 Boston Way
Lanham, MD 20706

3 Henrietta Street
London WC2E 8LU England

Preface

MANY WESTERN INTELLECTUALS AND RELIGIOUS LEADERS show a remarkable capacity to disbelieve the words and overlook the deeds of our sworn adversaries. At the same time, they find it easy to swallow the Big Lie or be lured by the Big Hope brandished by the propaganda merchants of an Adolf Hitler or a Joseph Stalin.

This striking capacity to accept the Big Lie and reject the Big Truth has been a persistent phenomena of twentieth century politics. Hitler's Reich, Stalin's Russia, and Gorbachev's Soviet Union, each brutal at home and expansionist abroad, have profited by those American and Western European intellectuals who have clung to the hollow promises of an exhausted ideology and refuse to see the jagged edges of a tyranny built on lies — the nightmarish claims of the Marxist-Leninist dream.

These "true believers," to use Eric Hoffer's telling phrase, have declined in number during the past two decades, a decline due less to new revelations about the evil empire than to the exposure of well-known outrages by card-carrying intellectuals, notably Alexander Solzhenitsyn. Mainstream Americans have had little difficulty in sensing the totalitarian threat because they are not afflicted with a sense of guilt about the success, wealth, and power of the United States. Their vision is not impaired by what Jeane Kirkpatrick has called the "blame America first" mentality.

The real or feigned fear of a nuclear Armageddon also feeds the tendency to ignore obvious facts and real dangers. The "better Red than dead" and peace-at-any-price viruses blind many otherwise rational persons to the threat of tyranny and aggression. Even before World War II, as Malcolm Muggeridge said with studied hyperbole: "All agreed that another war was unthinkable, unspeakable, inconceivable, and must at all costs be averted."

Add to all this the American tradition of isolationism and one can see that the revulsion against taking prudent measures against the most obvious external dangers will not be easily overcome. This paradoxical blend of innocence, nordinate fear, denial, and excessive self-doubt distorts the values and accomplishments of the West. The debilitating malaise that results cannot be cured by facts or rational argument alone. The cure requires experience, personal or vicarious.

In the essays that follow, three remarkable men—Sidney Hook, Vladimir Bukovsky, and Paul Hollander—each speaking from personal experience, make a strong case for facing the reality they have faced, and for translating prudential fear into responsible action.

Born in 1902, Sidney Hook was in the 1930s a brilliant exponent of Marxism. When he became disillusioned with Stalin's totalitarian tactics, he emerged as one of America's most perceptive critics of Communism. Vladimir Bukovsky endured twelve years in Soviet prisons, work camps, and psychiatric wards before being expelled from Russia. Paul Hollander was born in Hungary where he experienced the evil faces of both Fascist and Communist totalitarianism. Their combined witness is a compelling testimony to the peril we face.

In the past two decades, Soviet leaders have demonstrated a new sophistication in playing on Western feelings of guilt, inadequacy, and hope. Though they did not wholly succeed in diverting attention from their invasion of Afghanistan or intimidation of Poland by launching their recent "peace" initiatives, they did succeed in manipulating articulate Western voices who opposed the deployment of the Pershing II and cruise missiles in Western Europe. This clearly demonstrates that Soviet hypocrisy and disinformation are still able to gain a small but influential academic, religious, and media audience in the Free World.

The message of these three authors is vital. In peacetime, democracies are by nature reluctant to accept the disciplines of preparedness and are slow to respond with military force, even when peace and freedom are at stake, unless the challenge has the shocking clarity of a Pearl Harbor.

Sidney Hook, Vladimir Bukovsky, and Paul Hollander—each with deep roots in the Old World speak with authority to the New. They know that the Soviet threat is real and dangerous, and that a failure of nerve and resolve in the New World may surrender the ground to the totalitarians and set back the cause of freedom, democracy, and human rights for decades.

Ernest W. Lefever

January 14, 1987

Contents

A History of Hypocrisy

SIDNEY HOOK

T HE SOVIET UNION HAS REPEATEDLY used peace as a political weapon. In
fact, the first instance was the Bolshevik Revolution itself. Lenin
promised "Peace, Land, and Bread," but his goal was not to create peace
between nations. Rather he aimed to launch a revolutionary civil war and,
if he succeeded, to install a dictatorship of the proletariat to be ad-
ministered by the dictatorship of the Communist Party.

The shameless duplicity of the Soviet regime was seen again in the
1930s. First, the Kremlin helped undermine the Weimar Republic in Germany and thus helped Hitler rise to power; then, when Stalin felt threatened by Hitler's regime, he ordered the creation of worldwide Leagues for
Peace and Democracy. Their goal was to rally men of good will in defense
of the Soviet Union. But no sooner did the Soviets sign the Ribbentrop-
Molotov Peace Pact of 1939 (which unleashed World War II) than they
directed their puppet peace groups in the West to oppose the United States'
efforts to rearm itself. They piously proclaimed their unbounded commitment to peace and cynically portrayed Western military preparedness as
provocative war-mongering.

The Soviet Union renewed its use of peace as a political weapon soon after World War II ended in 1945. Resuming its Cold War against the West,
the Kremlin organized a series of lavish congresses and conferences osten-
sibly to promote the cause of world peace. But its actual goal was to con-
demn the foreign policy of the United States, to denounce NATO (which
was created after the Communist Warsaw Pact had been launched), and to
oppose the Marshall Plan for the rehabilitation of Europe.

Simultaneously, the Kremlin agitated for universal adoption of the
Stockholm Peace Pledge, but it abruptly switched its stance when South
Korea was invaded by the Communist regime in North Korea. At that mo-

---

SIDNEY HOOK, the well-known American philosopher and writer, has for several
decades been a leader in combating Communist and totalitarian influences in in-
tellectual life.

1

ment, conveniently, Pablo Picasso's "dove of peace," selected as the symbol of the Soviet-led world peace movement, was locked away in its cage.

For those with short memories or naive enough to believe that the Soviet Union's desire for peace is genuine, it is necessary to note that the Soviet Union rejected out-of-hand the Baruch-Lilienthal Peace Plan in which the United States offered to surrender its monopoly of atomic weapons to an international agency that would then supervise the use of atomic energy only for peaceful purposes. Every member of the United Nations recognized the magnanimity of this offer and voted to accept it; the only opponents were the Soviet Union and its satellites. By strict majority rule, of course, the Baruch-Lilienthal Peace Plan would have been adopted, but the Soviet Union exercised its veto to kill the proposal.

OTHER USES OF PEACE

If, up to now, I have seemed to imply that the Soviet Union was the only nation to use peace as a political weapon, let me set the record straight. During the early 1930s, Adolf Hitler repeatedly proclaimed his devotion to peace; at the same time he was flagrantly rearming Germany, in defiance of the 1919 Versailles Peace Treaty. Just as Lenin and Stalin managed to bamboozle a continuing stream of dupes, so Hitler succeeded too. Many pacifist groups took Hitler's paeans to peace as genuine expressions of his deepest beliefs, and they thereby aided him by opposing England's rearmament. The young men who took the Oxford Pledge – declaring they would refuse to serve King and Country in wartime – may have thought they were promoting peace. In fact, they were virtually guaranteeing war, because if England had rearmed earlier, Hitler might have been deterred from marching into the Rhineland, or seizing Czechoslovakia, or joining the Soviet Union in attacking Poland, the act of aggression that precipitated World War II.

Some readers may be impatient with my citing repeated instances of how the Soviets used peace as a political weapon. The past has no bearing on the present, they might claim, because the potential use of nuclear weapons makes history entirely irrelevant. According to this fashionable view, nuclear weapons pose dangers so great and so unprecedented that we must be prepared to risk or sacrifice anything in order to reduce the danger of nuclear annihilation. The obvious question to ask these passionate partisans of peace is: do their specific recommendations actually diminish the danger, or do they unwittingly increase it?

Vladimir Bukovsky has addressed precisely this question. He shows conclusively that those in the West who have failed to link the recognition of human rights with the struggle for peace, out of fear of the possible consequences of conflict, are increasing the very dangers they dread.

Bukovsky's analysis can hardly be improved upon. I add a few supplementary observations.

I would like to pose three questions to those who refuse to couple the issue of peace with issues of human rights. What would their attitude have been if Hitler had developed nuclear weapons? In the light of Hitler's record of treaty violations and his declared objectives, should we have lowered our guard or agreed to a weapons freeze with no other safeguards or assurances except his solemn promise to do the same? In the light of Hitler's gruesome practices and the evidence that in the event of victory he was prepared to carry them out on a worldwide scale, would those today who thoughtlessly chant "Better Red than Dead" have proclaimed "Better Nazi than Dead"?

All varieties of unilateral disarmament tend to present the basic choice the West faces as either being Red or Dead. Bukovsky regards this false alternative as being both foolish and illusory—foolish because intelligent opposition and resistance to Communist totalitarianism need not necessarily result in a universal holocaust, and illusory because abject capitulation to nuclear blackmail would not guarantee anyone's survival. In the world in which the Soviet Union has threatened to use nuclear weapons against Communist China, those who choose to be Red, rather than Dead, may end up first Red and then Dead.

DEFENDING FREEDOM

Bukovsky's criticism of the policy of appeasement suggests how we can have a world that is neither Red nor Dead. If the West wishes to preserve its freedom and resist the futher expansion of Soviet hegemony, it must retain a defense force strong enough to deprive the Soviet Union of the certainty of military victory. And before entering into agreements on significant arms reductions, the West also must insist that the Soviet Union implement the obligations it assumed under the Helsinki Accords and the United Nations Declaration of Human Rights.

Today, when the Kremlin uses the peace movement as a political weapon, it has a clear objective: it seeks to undermine the West's military capacity to withstand Communist aggression or threats of nuclear destruction. So long as that capacity remains unaffected, the Soviet Union will not risk war. Recall that before World War II broke out, it was widely predicted that because of the quantities of poison gas possessed by both sides, a war would make the planet uninhabitable. Yet we know that to the very end Hitler did not dare use poison gas because he realized the retaliatory actions it would provoke. And Hitler was a madman! By comparison, the Communist leaders are rational and hard-headed, and are well aware that unless the peace movement undermines the will of the West to resist Soviet aggression, they cannot move against the West with impunity.

Much of the discussion about verifying agreements with the Soviet Union has been misleading. First, there has been a tendency to exaggerate the extent to which significant violations of agreements can be detected by purely technical means. Second, the profound difference between the open society of the West and the completely closed system of the Soviet Union has been underestimated. Everyone, including the Kremlin, knows that if the United States enters into international agreements the force of independent public opinion assures that it will live up to them. In a free and open society, any treaty violation would be reported by an army of whistle-blowers to a press that is completely independent of the government. But if the Kremlin violates the provision of any agreement, as it has so often in the past, who will report it, and where? The news of the Chernobyl nuclear disaster got out only because of its effects on foreign nations. The Soviet Union is not only a closed society but has absolute control of the greatest land area in the world. All sorts of military activities can be conducted out of reach or sight of our latest instruments of detection. That is why if the provisions of the Helsinki Accords were implemented and if Soviet citizens were given the human rights that citizens of the West possess, the safeguards of compliance with agreements by the Soviet regime would be enormously strengthened.

Bukovsky has said that until the Soviet people enjoy the modicum of human rights promised under the Helsinki Accords and Soviet citizens are no longer ruthlessly punished in their efforts to exercise those rights, no agreements with the Soviet Union on disarmament or weapons control can be relied on. This is the wisdom of Andrei Sakharov's warning to the West and to the politically innocent members of the Western peace movements who are holding their own governments responsible for the periodic tensions produced by the Soviet regime in Afghanistan and other areas of the world.

In the absence of any perceptible progress in the area of human rights in the Soviet Union, the best safeguard of Western freedom is the development of a defense capacity strong enough to deter the Soviet Union from unleashing war. For there are weighty historical, psychological and ideological reasons why, unless it is attacked, the Soviet Union will never undertake a war it is not certain to win.

What Are These Reasons?

First, the Communists worship at the altar of history. It makes no sense to them to risk survival, even in a good cause. Nothing exists for them except this world and unless war is forced on them, as it was by Hitler, they will not undertake it, unless they are certain that their potential victims (as was the case in Poland, Hungary, and Afghanistan) cannot exact unacceptable costs. Whenever confronted by a resolute and powerful opponent whose defeat they cannot easily predict, they will retreat, as they did at the time of the Berlin blockade and the Cuban missile crisis.

Secondly, the Soviets are unlikely to undertake a war they are not certain to win because, although they still regard the existence of other, especially free, cultures as a threat to their own existence, they are convinced they can overcome these threats without war. What they regard as "the correlation of world forces" favors them. There is some justification for their belief. All we need do is to compare the maps of the world at the outbreak of the Bolshevik Revolution and the maps of the world in 1939, 1945, and today. Not a single Communist gain, despite its forcible imposition, has been reversed. On the contrary, the Kremlin has proclaimed the Brezhnev Doctrine: no nation in which Communists have seized power can be permitted to liberate itself from the yoke of Communist rule. Authoritarian regimes in Spain, Portugal, and Greece and dictatorships in South America have won their way back to democratic rule. But no Communist regime has evolved into a democracy. The halting and premature steps, taken first in Hungary, then in Czechoslovakia, were forcibly repressed by the Soviet Union.

The very advance of Communism on a world scale is evidence that its expansion cannot be interpreted merely as a geopolitical continuation of Czarist foreign policy. Czarist Russia often sent its armies into the heartland of Europe but always remained on its periphery. It never used proxies and client states as the Kremlin has done to venture into Africa, Central America, and Indochina.

The third reason that the Soviet Union is unlikely to wage a war for world hegemony unless it is certain of victory is that its leaders still profess a belief in their ideological dogmas. Therefore they expect that the societies of the West will sooner or later collapse, due to the "contradictions" in their economies, which ultimately spell bankruptcy. The Soviet economy is in a state of permanent crisis, which its leaders hope to resolve by absorbing the technological skills and know-how of the declining West, peacefully if possible, and by threat of nuclear blackmail if the West's will to resist can be undermined by peace movements that unwittingly serve as instruments of Soviet foreign policy.

No man can have more peace than his neighbor will allow him. We can honor and respect the individual who regards violence as so evil that in his effort to prevent it, he lays down his life. But if what is at stake is not *his* life or freedom, but the lives and freedom of *others* who are threatened by the violence of aggressors, one must be more or less than human to do nothing, rather than to resist the aggression.

Sometimes the very willingness and ability to resist aggression is the best insurance against the necessity of having to do so. Winston Churchill regarded World War II as an unnecessary war because under the influence of pacifist sentiment in the West, cynically encouraged by Nazis, a policy of appeasement was adopted that encouraged Hitler to risk going into battle.

Today the Soviet Union seeks to disarm the free world through a massive campaign of devotion to peace at all costs. The Soviets entice the citizens of the West to participate in these campaigns while forbidding any *independent, non-governmental* group within their own borders to agitate for the same measures.

War is a terrible and ugly thing under any circumstances. But as the wars for freedom and survival against barbaric cruelty show from Genghis Khan to Hitler, mankind has recognized that there are some things even worse than war. What makes life worth living is more than mere life itself. John Stuart Mill restated a truth known to the wise men and women of all cultures: "A man who has nothing which he cares about more than he does his personal safety is a miserable creature who has no chance of being free, unless made and kept so by the existence of better men than himself." The future is not foreordained: the West need not resign itself to the inevitability of Soviet rule. But the West can remain free and secure only if it possesses the intelligence and courage to defend itself—and to recognize the utter futility of appeasement and cowardice.

Peace as a Political Weapon

VLADIMIR BUKOVSKY

NO MATTER HOW MUCH EVIDENCE is amassed of Soviet deception during the past thirty years—violation of international agreements, manipulation of public opinion, subversion and terrorism, covert coups and overt aggression—a large part of the Western public still finds it too difficult to accept. If nothing else, the sheer scope of this Soviet activity and the utterly inhuman methods they employ make a "balanced" Western observer suspicious.

Even the most undeniable facts—like shooting down the Korean Airliner, or the invasion of Afghanistan—failed to change public opinion in the West. Instead, the very absurdity of Soviet behavior in both cases has prompted many people to look for a more "rational" explanation of Soviet motives, or even for a justification. And more often than not, these explanations tend to blame the Western governments rather than the Soviets.

Unfortunately, such an attitude is only natural. Any textbook of medical psychology describes a similar pattern of behavior displayed by a mother who lost her child, or by a patient with terminal cancer. In general, whenever a person is confronted with something mind-boggling, something utterly horrible and beyond his control, he goes through a succession of mental states ranging from denial to guilt, and from fantastic "rationalization" to acute depression.

Indeed, what can be more traumatic than to face a mortal enemy who stops at nothing and who can destroy the earth five times over? An enemy who subjugates country after country, slowly but steadily, for half a century; who penetrates every sphere of our life and ruthlessly exploits our every weakness—all for no apparent reason? In the course of history, the West has tried practically every possible approach, from containment to

VLADIMIR BUKOVSKY spent twelve years in Soviet prisons, work camps, and psychiatric hospitals before being expelled from Russia. He has published an autobiography, *To Build a Castle: My Life as a Dissenter*, and writes frequently on Western misconceptions of the Soviet Union. A shorter version of this essay first appeared in *Ethics, Deterrence, and National Security*, published by the Institute for Foreign Policy Analysis.

détente, and nothing has worked. As Solzhenitsyn suggests, the Soviet specter is like a cancer and, therefore, not surprisingly, our reaction to it is similar to that of a cancer patient.

Soviet behavior, however, ceases to appear so frighteningly irrational and unbelievably cruel as soon as we understand that they regard themselves as being at war with the rest of the world. Basically, we accept different moral standards during wartime, and many acts of violence and deception appear justified. Thus, the sinking of the Lusitania by German U-boats in 1915 was probably a worse crime than shooting down a passenger airliner in 1983, simply because the former incident killed at least four times as many innocent people and because it occurred in neutral waters, while the latter occurred within Soviet air space. Yet we are inclined to accept the sinking as legitimate, while the airline incident is viewed as a totally irrational and inexplicable act.

Similarly, when we read about Lawrence of Arabia, we are not particularly outraged by his skillful manipulation of feuding Arab tribes. Yet we refuse to believe that the Soviets routinely employ the same methods of warfare by supporting and manipulating all kinds of extremist groups around the world. The facts are undeniable, but it seems just too mean to be true.

And, speaking of propaganda, have deception or disinformation, not always been legitimate means of war, from the Trojan horse to the fake D-Day assaults? Every country's army has a special detachment for psychological warfare, dormant in peacetime and activated at the beginning of hostilities. The only difference in the case of the Soviet Union is that the entire country became such a detachment, while the war itself was not formally declared.

Strictly speaking, however, we can not blame the Soviets even for waging an undeclared war against humanity: this war was actually proclaimed at the turn of the century by the founders of Marxist-Leninist ideology under the banner of "class struggle" and it continues unabated ever since. Every five years at each Communist Party Congress, the Soviet ruling clique solemnly reaffirms the declaration of war by pledging its full support to "liberation movements" and to the "forces of progress and socialism."

THE SAME IDEOLOGICAL STATE

Sixty years after Lenin's death, the Soviet Union remains the same ideological state serving the purposes of the world revolution as he had conceived it. It does not matter that no one nowadays believes in Communist dogma. In their everyday lives the Soviet people may perceive it as a nuisance, or as a source of numerous jokes shared equally by the people and their rulers. But at the end of the day, the Communist Party is still in firm control of every aspect of Soviet life, and Communist ideology is never challenged within the Party. The differences between the Communist and non-Communist worlds are still defined as "antagonistic" (i.e. irreconcilable), as are those between the opposing "classes" of "capitalist society"—the proletariat and bourgeoisie.

What was once a utopia, a dream, became a structure, an institution, and an everyday job for millions of people. The Soviet Union is not a state in the traditional meaning of the word, but a huge and well-organized army of ideological warriors, a fortress with hundreds of front organizations, thousands of publications around the world, and with a gigantic budget, perhaps even a bigger one than their military budget.

The idea of a permanent war against the non-Communist world is the dominant feature of Soviet life. As in Nazi Germany, millions are brought up in the spirit of militarism and hatred, convinced by the pervasive propaganda that every foreigner is a spy, an enemy by definition. Just as one example of this massive militaristic upbringing, look at a copy of a popular Soviet magazine for pre-school children, *"Veselye Kartinki"* (Merry Pictures). With a circulation of *9,000,000* copies, it is dedicated to glorification of the military tradition, past and present, to praising the Soviet Army in general and the border guards in particular, because "they protect your peaceful and happy childhood." In the light of this, should we be surprised that the murder of some three hundred people on a Korean airliner did not arouse popular indignation in the Soviet Union?

Consistent with a state of permanent war is notorious Soviet secretiveness. Practically anything, from a small-scale map to a telephone directory, or from the production goals of a factory to statistics of accidents and natural disasters, is treated as an official secret. Recently a new law was passed making it a criminal offense (punishable by three years in labor camps) to pass virtually any information to a foreigner or to any person who just might pass it to a foreigner. This new law, of course, does not apply to passing genuine military information, the penalty for which has always been the firing squad.

In fact, the Soviet system not only stresses secretiveness, but a deliberately cultivated paranoia. Numerous TV series about foreign spies, endless films about World War II, persistent official appeals for vigilance, and artificially created international tensions – all these are designed to maintain a spirit of mobilization and virtually a state of martial law.

Not surprisingly, any attempt by a Soviet citizen to escape to a "capitalist country" (or a refusal to return from a visit to such a country) is treated under Soviet law as high treason and is equated with desertion by a soldier to enemy forces during a war (article 64, part 3 of the Penal Code of the Russian Federation).

PATRIOTIC DECEPTIONS

In such a political atmosphere it became only natural that if, by any chance, an ordinary Soviet man comes into contact with a foreigner, his patriotic duty is to deceive the "enemy." Thus, entire streets are freshly painted, roads are paved and red carpets are laid down in anticipation of a foreign delegation at every town, collective farm, school, or factory it is supposed to visit. "Occasional encounters" (allegedly accidental and spontaneous) are rehearsed well in advance. Food and consumer goods are urgently brought and displayed in shop windows. Potential trouble-makers are jailed, or locked up in lunatic asylums, or simply sent away under a suitable pretext. And woe be to them who may spoil the picture of prosperous and peaceful Soviet life.

Equally, those who are allowed to travel abroad on official business (or as tourists) are instructed what to say and what to do. Special KGB agents are placed among them to monitor their performances, while their families back home serve as hostages. A Soviet man travelling abroad is not a civilian, but a frontline soldier in the ongoing ideological war.

One might say that these methods are too crude to deceive anybody. Yet, the sheer scope of this deception is simply too huge for many to become suspicious. An average Western man is not prepared to detect a colossal and audacious falsification. Let us remember that an outrageous falsification was actually believed by millions in the West for many decades. In the darkest hours of Stalin's great terror, Western intellectuals were praising his regime as the most just and humane on earth, and they were greeting it as the harbinger of mankind's bright future. The trend has changed only very recently, when thousands of refugees came, wave after wave, from Hungary, Czechoslovakia, Poland, and the Soviet Union, bringing their stories of horror. Only after dozens of books were published disclosing the truth about the Soviet regime (like Solzhenitsyn's *Gulag Archipelago*), only after the truth about persecution of Jews and the abuse of psychiatry for political purposes became widely known, while application of the Communist model created obvious disasters everywhere, from Cambodia and Vietnam, to Ethiopia and Angola, to Cuba and Nicaragua — only then did the "crude" methods of the overt Soviet propaganda cease to be effective.

Still, many thousands of those who visited the Soviet Union recently came out with the impression that the Soviets, whatever problems they might have (and who has no problems?) are essentially just another country, not too different from the rest of the world, and certainly do not want a war with anybody. Thus, the main goal of the Soviet disinformation — to conceal the fact of war waged by them against the non-Communist world — is still being pursued. As Dr. Goebbels, an early expert in the field, once said: "A lie must be monstrous to be convincing."

THE BRAINWASHING CAMPAIGN

Robert Gillette in his *Los Angeles Times* article (August 12, 1984) from Moscow, "Soviets Show the Facade of Peace," describes in detail the massive brainwashing campaign:

Two centuries later *pokazukha* [the façade] is alive and well in Russia, and an integral part of state propaganda. Its principal targets today are the growing numbers of American and West European peace activists who come here in organized tours to see for themselves whether the Soviet Union is, as it claims to be, a benign and peace loving nation.

Some return home discouraged by the heavy-handedness of Soviet propaganda and the inflexibility of officials who uniformly insist that "American imperialism" is the sole cause of tension in the world.

But hundreds of others, whose fears of a nuclear holocaust seemingly predispose them to take Soviet reassurances of good will at face value, come away from whirlwind tours with a glowing image of the country and its ambitions in the world arena that bears little resemblance to the Soviet Union familiar to the foreign scholars, diplomats, journalists, and businessmen who live here.

Although their numbers are relatively small, the often bizarre image they carry away is amplified by the dozens of speeches many will deliver back home to church and civic groups across the United States, with cumulative audiences numbering in the tens of thousands.

Many of the peace tours are hosted by the official Soviet Peace Committee, an arm of the propaganda of the Communist Party's Central Committee, headed by Yuri Zhukov, a veteran political commentator at

Pravda, the main Party newspaper. Zhukov is an alternative member of the Central Committee.

On the American side, the names of groups sponsoring peace tours of the Soviet Union reflect their hopes that a grass-roots dialogue with "ordinary Russians" will somehow succeed in easing tensions where conventional diplomacy has failed.

"US–USSR Bridges for Peace" in Norwich, Vermont, for instance, brings leaders of nuclear freeze groups from New England communities. "US–USSR Citizens Dialogue" gathers up ordinary Americans from across the country for a whirlwind exposure to Russian hospitality.

A Woodmont, Connecticut, organization called "Promoting Enduring Peace, Inc.," which describes itself as non-political as well as non-profit, takes a more leisurely approach. The group sponsors summertime "peace cruises" down the Volga on a luxury ship that its promotional literature calls the "Dove Boat." From the moment they arrive in Leningrad or Moscow until their departure ten days to two weeks later, the jet-lagged Americans are plunged into an exhausting round of banquets, peace seminars, state-sponsored peace rallies, factory visits, folk concerts, and glimpses of the pomp and glitter of Russian Orthodox Church services.

Some Americans are suprised to see Russians on the streets behaving like ordinary people, chatting, often smiling, coddling their children. When these fleeting scenes of Soviet life fail to match up with the Orwellian image of a repressive state many Westerners bring with them, they conclude—with encouragement from their Soviet hosts—that the deception lies on the other side.

The visitors' horizons are further limited by the fact that almost none of them speak Russian. Even those who do seem generally unaware that most Soviet citizens, when confronted by an unknown and inquisitive foreigner, find it best to respond with a faithful reproduction of Pravda or the last obligatory political lecture he or she attended.

Travelling in the company of polished and gregarious Soviet journalists and selected tour guides who speak colloquial American English, the visitors hear endless toasts to *mir i druzhba*—peace and friendship. Often, there is a visit to a model elementary school where brightly dressed children present flowers to the foreigners, then join hands with them and sing "We Shall Overcome."

"We garden-variety Americans aren't accustomed to walking into an auditorium where the whole school applauds us," Wayne Bryan of San Antonio, Texas, who was on a "Citizens Dialogue" tour, told a Moscow news conference. "We held hands all around and sang 'We Shall Overcome.' It was a very moving experience."

The tours of schools and children's camps carefully avoid glimpses of compulsory civil defense and military education for boys and girls.

The touring Americans, many of whom see themselves as practicing an alternative diplomacy, resent being told by diplomats and other resident foreigners here that their Soviet travelling companions are not journalists and peace activists in the Western sense, but propagandists—a legitimate profession in Soviet terms, with no invidious connotation—whose business is not to inform public opinion but to guide it.

"We were overcome by the warmth of the welcome, by the tears, by the cry for peace in such difficult times," Helen Hamilton, a Presbyterian peace activist from Tacoma, Washington, said after a tour that included a visit with Valentina Tereshkova, the imposing former cosmonaut who heads the Soviet Women's Committee.

"She may not be as free as I am to work for peace, but she is not a propagandist," Hamilton said with indignation in her voice when a reporter suggested that Tereshkova's job was mainly one of public relations with Western women's groups.

In city after city, the visitors file through war memorials where they are told that a nation that lost 20 million people in World War II could not possibly harbor aggressive aims towards others.

Few foreign visitors seem to sense that they have stepped into a torrent of domestic peace propaganda designed to convince ordinary Russians—who do indeed want peace—that the state's massive military investments are vital not only to protect the Soviet homeland, but to preserve world stability and the "gains of socialism" across the globe, from Vietnam to Cuba, and from Afghanistan to Poland.

The peace tours often end with a "plenary session" and a news conference in the spacious wood-paneled headquarters of the Soviet Peace Committee, which is located fittingly on *Prospect Mira*—Peace Avenue.

Under the warm glow of television lights, Soviet reporters from Radio Moscow, Tass, and the Novosti press agency pose questions that elicit expressions of gratitude from the Americans for the warmth and hospitality they have seen and that encourage them to believe they are now part of a vital link between East and West.

Anne Swallow, for example, a minister from Carmel Valley, California, who led a United Church of Christ delegation from Northern California and Nevada in June, told one such news conference that she and her group were "gratified to have been part of breaking down the wall of mistrust."

Although members of the group had spent only two weeks on a busy tour, she said they came away with a "better appreciation of the incredible diversity in religion, culture, and even ideology" that seemed to exist in the Soviet Union.

Most seem to emerge from the pressure-cooker of Russian hospitality convinced, despite the anti-American propaganda they acknowledge having heard along the way, that they have taken part in a meaningful grass-roots dialogue that has begun to chip away at the "misunderstanding" they believe lies at the heart of U.S.–Soviet tensions.

"We are by no means a group of tourists," Clinton Gardner, a founder of Bridges for Peace, told a Moscow press conference earlier this year. "We have made a breakthrough . . . in a new style of dialogue between nations. I feel that Soviet society is ready to work with us."

Touring Western peace activists often voice indignation at suggestions that they are being used, but their visits do serve Soviet interests in several ways.

For one, they lead to reciprocal visits to the United States and Western Europe by Soviet journalists, churchmen, and Peace Committee officials whose Western hosts often present them, in sincerity, as ordinary Russians.

Moreover, visiting Westerners lend credence and legitimacy to domestic Soviet propaganda as they travel about the country, giving interviews at every stop to local journalists. Russians are as wary of propaganda as any people, but when they hear visiting foreigners praising the strength and unanimity of the Soviet peace "movement" and the peaceable aims of Moscow's foreign policy, they are more likely to listen.

The Soviet Peace Committee has convinced many of its guests that, despite its faithful reflection of government views, it is not an "official" organization but the focal point of a grass-roots disarmament movement roughly comparable to those in the West. This false impression appears to ease the apprehensions some American and European nuclear freeze advocates feel about putting unilateral pressure on their own governments.

"It is wrong to call this an 'official' organization, because its money comes from voluntary donations, not the state," Clinton Gardner of Bridges for Peace, among others, has insisted.

The voluntary nature of these donations can be seen regularly on Soviet television news. A party lecturer harangues a crowd of lethargic, blank-faced factory workers standing on the shop floor. Someone on the podium calls for donating a day's wages to the Peace Committee. The right arms of the workers rise in unison and the proposal carries without dissent. Russians, at least, understand that to vote "no," however much one might favor peace, would only invite needless trouble.

I have reproduced this lengthy quotation simply because it gives the best description of the Soviet machinery of peace ever to appear in the Western press. It shows how the good intentions of people in the East and West are used to confuse and deceive each other, thus making them unwilling instruments of Soviet ideological warfare. Nobody is required to believe in the ideological dogma anymore. It is quite sufficient to have, on the one hand, an inexhaustible desire to be deceived, while, on the other hand, an equally unlimited willingness to submit, in order to make a powerful political weapon out of people's desire to live in peace.

THE STRUGGLE FOR PEACE AS A SOVIET FOREIGN POLICY TOOL

Before examining the most recent developments in the peace movement, let me briefly reiterate the main positions set forth in my pamphlet in 1981, *The Peace Movement and the Soviet Union.*[1] Contrary to the allegations made by those who apparently did not read my pamphlet carefully, and yet have taken it upon themselves to criticize it, I did not ascribe the emergence of the peace movement in Europe to a "Communist conspiracy." In fact, exactly the opposite is true: the "struggle for peace" has always been a cornerstone of Soviet foreign policy, a position openly proclaimed and inscribed in all Communist Party resolutions. According to Soviet ideology, real lasting peace can only be achieved by destroying capitalism, that "hotbed of contradictions and imperialist intentions." Why, they ask themselves, should brother-proletarians want to kill each other once they are free from "capitalist oppression"?

Moreover, according to their ideology, the ultimate triumph of Communism in the world is historically inevitable, which means they do not need to initiate a world war unless they are certain they will win it. Of course, history must be encouraged and helped a bit now and then. Thus, a war fought in the "interests of the proletariat" is considered to be a "just war," because, they believe, it leads to the liberation of humanity from the "chains of capitalism," a development that ultimately will save mankind from the evils of war.

In practical terms, the "struggle for peace" has always been a useful tool of Soviet foreign policy. Communists have always known very well that the majority of the population in any country of the world would accept their rule only as a last resort—only when the alternative would be absolutely unbearable. They are, therefore, very skillful in exploiting unbearable situations (or in creating them, as in Poland), and they are extremely clever at molding political events to give the appearance that their rule is the only alternative. Thus, opponents appear to be "unreasonable" and "enemies of peace," while the Communists are the "peacemakers."

Besides, in the ideological struggle it is much more advantageous to be on the side of such noble causes as "justice," "peace," "equality"—a terminological game played by the Soviets to the point of perfection. So, they are indeed "peace-lovers," if we are to accept their definition of peace.

One can find plenty of examples in recent history to confirm the consistency of the Soviets' "peaceful" policy as described above—the creation of the Soviet Union itself out of the ashes of World War I, and the turmoil of the subsequent civil war, Moscow's "love affair" with Hitler, and the events during World War II. After the war, they touted the cause of peace while trying to catch up with the West in the nuclear arms race and as a means to silence the public outcry over their occupation of Eastern Europe. And now, as they try to retain their nuclear superiority over the West, they use it again to silence the growing criticism of Soviet adventurism in the Third World and of human rights violations at home. Finally, and perhaps most importantly, they exploit the cause of peace to extend their political influence in Western Europe. Once again political foes of the Soviet Union—this time the Western democracies—are defamed as "unreasonable," as "insane," or as "warmongers" just because they do not want to accept the "lesser evil" of Soviet domination as an alternative to the ultimate evil of nuclear holocaust.

Also, contrary to the hysterical outcry of many anti-nuclear activists, I did not imply in the 1981 pamphlet that the so-called peace movement consists exclusively of paid Soviet agents. In fact, I had taken the trouble to repeat at least four times within fifty pages that in my view the overwhelming majority of peace marchers are well-intentioned, albeit confused, naive, and frightened people. As usual, there are plenty of professional political profiteers who seek popularity by jumping on the bandwagon of peace at any price, just as there are plenty of people who try to exploit the atmosphere of panic for their own selfish purposes. But there is also not the slightest doubt that this motley crowd is manipulated by a handful of activists instructed directly from Moscow.

Conclusive Evidence

There were already quite a few facts available by the end of 1981 to prove the latter conclusion. To begin with, the peace movement's onesidedness itself was very revealing. The major constituent groups of the movement have conspicuously refrained from condemning Soviet imperialism in Afghanistan, Poland, and other places, just as they have refused to denounce Soviet violations of international treaties and human rights agreements. They were crying shame on the Americans for merely planning to develop and deploy weapons like the enhanced radiation warhead and the cruise and Pershing missiles, but they were speaking only in whispers of the hundreds of Soviet SS-20s already aimed at Europe. They were happily throwing stones at General Haig in Germany, but Marshal Brezhnev did not provoke similar outbursts of anger.

There were, moreover, a number of reports on the heavy representation of Communists in the leadership of the major peace groups, representation that was disproportionate to their number in the rank-and-file. There were also occasional quarrels inside the peace movement over the existence of Communist influence on decision-making, and there were even a few instances of direct Soviet involvement, as in the case of Arne Petersen in Denmark.

But most of the evidence of Soviet involvement in the European peace movement could easily be found by reading the Soviet newspapers and by comparing them with major peace movement publications. The new slogans adopted in Moscow would normally take from one to six months to migrate into major peace movement publications in Western Europe. The swiftness with which this occurred suggests a close, if somewhat indirect, link between some peace movement leaders and the masters of the Kremlin. The most striking example of West European peace activists following the Soviet lead was the designation of the last week in October as the target date for staging large peace rallies in Europe. This decision was first made public during the "World Parliament of Peoples for Peace" in Sofia, Bulgaria, in September 1980. Within a month, the first large anti-nuclear demonstrations took place in West European capitals.

It is also possible to trace the origin of the current peace campaign to specific Soviet actions. According to Soviet newspaper reports, the actual decision to begin supporting peace activists in the West was taken in the summer of 1979, more than a year before it was finally launched in Sofia. One can easily reconstruct the reasoning that led to this decision. If we keep in mind that since 1977 the Soviets have been deploying SS-20s at a rate of one per week, we should have no difficulty in realizing how helpful a peace movement in Western Europe could be in thwarting Western efforts to match the Soviet nuclear arms buildup in kind. There was, moreover, the need to preclude Western criticism of the Soviet invasion of Afghanistan, which occurred about the same time the Kremlin decided to become involved in peace movements in the West. It was not difficult at the time for the Soviets to imagine what the West's reaction to these moves would be. It may mean the end of détente, they probably thought, but they knew that they could always resort to their traditional cold war strategy of combining provocations with the ever-present Soviet "struggle for peace."

The Peace Conference in Bulgaria

After a year of active preparations, the initial stages of the peace campaign were remarkably successful. The "peace conference" in Bulgaria in September 1980 attracted 2,260 delegates from 137 countries, who claimed to represent 330 political parties, 100 international associations, and over 3,000 national non-governmental organizations. To be sure, this was no ordinary meeting of the international Communist movement. The political spectrum of those represented was exceptionally wide: 200 members of different national parliaments, 200 trade-union leaders, 129 leading Social Democrats (33 of them members of their respective national executive bodies), 150 writers and poets, 33 representatives of different liberation movements, women's organizations, youth organizations, the World Council of Churches and other religious organizations, 18 representatives of different U.N. specialized committees, representatives of the Organization of African Unity and of OPEC, retired military officers, and representatives of 83 Communist parties.[2]

To gather such a wide variety of people from so many different political backgrounds to attend a political conference in a Communist country is by no means an easy task. The possibility that their presence might be interpreted as an endorsement of the Soviet Union's aggressive and oppressive policies would normally deter many of them from coming. In the past even some Communist parties would have hesitated to send their representatives. What happened on this occasion, however, was simply unbelievable: these 2,260 people voted unanimously to approve the absolutely pro-Soviet "Charter of the Peoples for Peace" and "Program for Action." How could this be possible in the wake of the Soviet occupation of Afghanistan, at a time when even many Western athletes had refused to participate in the Moscow Olympics?

Of course, one might guess that these "representatives" were quite carefully chosen in advance (after all, the Soviets had more than a year for preparations), and that only those known to be particularly "soft" on the peace issue were invited. Still, that alone could not have secured such a stunning success. To be sure, the gathering was convened not by the Soviet government or by a Communist party, but by the World Peace Council. Who does not know, however, that this Council is a Soviet front organization? Moreover, the venue was carefully chosen—it was Bulgaria, not Czechoslovakia, or East Germany, let alone the Soviet Union. Still, who on earth could believe that Bulgaria would arrange an international conference independently from their Soviet masters?

THE SOVIET USE OF THE "ABSOLUTE VALUE"

The reason for the success of this conference is simply that the Soviets are extremely skilled at brainwashing people. One of their most successful tricks, the same one which is the very foundation of Communist ideology, is to confront a human being with an "absolute value." Thus, the Soviets tout an absolute and everlasting happiness for mankind as an irresistibly appealing ideal attainable only through Communism. Similarly, the absolute and irreversible destruction of the entire globe, horrible as it is shown to be in numerous documentaries, is another "absolute value," only this time an absolutely negative one. Relativism is a difficult concept to grasp, let alone to live with. Absolute value, on the other hand, whether positive or negative, saves us from the spiritual anguish of having to choose constantly between good and better, between bad and worse. But it also deprives us of our free will. It enslaves us.

This subject is endless, and it is not my task here to plunge into an extended philosophical essay. But a comment is in order on the notorious decision by American Catholic bishops to declare that nuclear weapons are immoral. Christian morality is a foundation of our civilization, and no one should think for a moment that the bishops have a monopoly on it. In my understanding, the Christian doctrine rejects simple arithmetic in the question of morality. Human life is proclaimed to be priceless, and one life is deemed to be as priceless as a dozen lives. Then, how can they calculate that nuclear war is immoral, while conventional war is not? After all, the conventional World War II cost humanity some 50 million lives. Was it moral or immoral to defend ourselves against Hitler's aggression?

As I have pointed out earlier, the absolute value deprives us of free will. As Sidney Hook quite rightly remarked, "Those who say that life is worth living at any cost have already written for themselves an epitaph of infamy, for there is no cause and no person that they will not betray to stay alive."[3] Indeed, such endorsement of immorality is very strange to hear from God's shepherds, who, after all, should be more concerned with a man's soul than with his survival.

Be that as it may, in practice it was precisely the psychological lure of the absolute value that lay behind the stunning success of Soviet propaganda in Sofia and elsewhere. In the name of the ultimate value, people were asked to betray their normal values. After sufficiently scaring them with the horrors of a possible nuclear holocaust, they were bluntly told that the West was pushing the world toward the edge of catastrophe by imposing economic sanctions on the Eastern bloc and by boycotting cultural exchanges and sporting events (in response, of course, to the Soviet invasion of Afghanistan and the persecution of scientists in the USSR). In order to defuse the issue of human rights, which was clearly putting them on the defensive, the Soviets proclaimed a new slogan: "The people have the power to preserve peace—their main right." Thus, in pursuit of the ultimate right, the people were supposed to sacrifice all other rights. And they did. After all, who cares how many are arrested, tortured, or killed by the Soviets when the main task is to save humanity from destruction? Not surprisingly, nobody asked the Soviets the most obvious questions: If you are as anxious to avoid a holocaust as you say, why should you continue to oppress your own people and others? Why should you remain in Afghanistan? Why should you not simply disarm unilaterally, as you require us to do? No, nobody asked these questions, because the Soviets are known to be "impossible," while the West is known to be only "unreasonable" and often amenable to pressure.

DIPLOMACY INSTEAD OF EMBARRASSING QUESTIONS

Instead of asking the Soviets embarrassing questions, people of quite different professions have suddenly become preoccupied with the craft of diplomacy. They have been mesmerized by the "absolute value" and frightened by Soviet threats, deployment of SS-20s, and walkouts from arms reduction talks. Thus, American hosts of an official Soviet delegation are indignant when somebody tries to ask their guests an awkward question about violations of human rights or about persecution of Jews in the Soviet Union. Such questions are considered undiplomatic and detrimental to U.S.–Soviet relations. Justifying his decision to renew scientific exchanges with the Soviet Union at the very moment when Dr. Andrei Sakharov was reportedly dying in exile, the President of the American National Academy of Science, Frank Press, asserted: "Despite our continuous concern for Sakharov, there are some issues of such deep importance to the future of mankind that we have felt it necessary to continue talking about them with our Soviet counterparts. In this regard, arms control and international security are certainly of high priority. Our members feel very strongly about this issue."[4]

A respected scholar with no sympathy for Communism, Professor John Kenneth Galbraith, suddenly presents his readers with a highly optimistic view of the Soviet economy and goes even so far as to suggest that the Soviet people earn too much. Why?

I am not attracted by the Soviet system, but I am committed to the need of arms control—to the thought that after a nuclear exchange the ashes of Communism will be indistinguishable from the ashes of capitalism, even by the most perceptive ideologist. But it is a prerequisite for the control of nuclear weapons that there be a modicum of confidence and trust between the two countries.[5]

Hence, on his recent "visit to Russia," he notices only similarities between the American and Soviet societies. He even gives his Soviet hosts advice on how to improve the image of Communism:

When, in the Soviet Union, the spendable income exceeds the available supplies of the more sought-after goods, queues form at the shop. We saw these one day as we drove past a large shopping center on the edge of Leningrad. Standing in a queue is an uncomfortable thing; the shortages that induce it are seen as a failure of the government or the system. I asked my hosts if it wouldn't be wiser to distribute a little less income in relation to the supply of goods, since wages, after all, are under state control. In consequence, people would attribute their inability to buy to their failure to earn enough rather than to the failure of the economic system to supply the desired goods. Surely, that would be better for the reputation of the system.[6]

As for the question of nuclear disarmament, this "is an effort one pursues primarily at home."[7]

SOVIET INFLUENCE OVER THE PEACE MOVEMENT

Once again, this time through the "peace movement," Soviet propaganda has managed to hoodwink a considerable number of people in the West. After taking a spiritual lead over the movement, it was not very difficult to take an organizational one. After all, if we are to accept the "peace at any price" philosophy, we must all unite irrespective of our past crimes, political differences, and beliefs in order to survive. That was precisely the message presented by the head of the Soviet "delegation," B. N. Ponomarev (Alternative Member of the Soviet Politburo and Head of the CPSU Central Committee's International Department), in a speech before the delegates to the Sofia conference. And it was accepted unanimously, not only by Soviet delegates, but by Westerners as well, by Catholic priests, social democrats, liberals, trade-unionists, and women's "lib" activists. For all our Western tolerance, is it still not shocking to see Westerners, no matter what their political cause, marching hand in hand with representatives of the Soviet Communist Party "to save humanity"?

What these multitudes of "inspired" people apparently do not know is that Communists are incapable of normal human cooperation—they are either your enemies, or they rule you. It is necessary only to look at what happened to the Labor Party in Britain to understand this simple fact.[8] Thus, in no time the small and nearly forgotten European Communist parties have taken over the leadership of the "peace movement" in Europe.

This fact has now, three years later, become common knowledge. In an article entitled, "The Story of Who's Behind Britain's CND,"[9] Douglas Eden reveals that there is a large proportion of members of the British Communist Party in the CND (Campaign for Nuclear Disarmament) conference leadership, and that even the resolutions of the CP's annual conferences are echoed by CND conference resolutions. More details of the Communist manipulation of the CND are set forth in an excellent article by Alun Chalfont in *Encounter*, and similar facts concerning Communist influence in the German and Dutch peace movements can be found in an article by Dr. Wynfred Joshua in *Strategic Review*.[10] The latter article also provides considerable information on the degree of direct Soviet involvement in the "peace movement" in the United States.

The evidence of direct Soviet involvement in the Western peace movement is so great that one could compile quite a lengthy catalog of facts and references. For example, in Switzerland, where Novosti Press Agency officials were discovered to be running the entire peace movement, the Swiss government closed the Bern bureau of Novosti, expelled the agency's bureau chief, and forced the withdrawal of a Soviet diplomat it said was a KGB officer responsible for overseeing Novosti's local operations. The Swiss Foreign Ministry lodged a stiff formal protest with the Soviet Embassy accusing Novosti of "continued, grave interference in Swiss affairs incompatible" with its normal functions in a neutral country. The strongly worded note and other official Swiss documents asserted that Novosti had been involved in political activities ranging from masterminding antinuclear demonstrations, organizing anti-American rallies, supervising one demonstration that actually took place inside the chambers of the Swiss Parliament, and purveying disinformation.[11]

While the Soviet escapade in Switzerland was handled firmly and consistently by the Swiss government, American officials mishandled the issue of Soviet influence in the U.S. "nuclear freeze" movement. Still suffering from an anti-"McCarthyism" complex, the FBI director promptly reassured puzzled Americans that there was absolutely no evidence to suggest that the Soviets were manipulating the American freeze movement, and this line was quickly echoed by the "intelligence community." One needs neither a community nor any great degree of intelligence to see, however, that the whole idea of a "nuclear freeze" originated in the Soviet Union, specifically with the personal appeal made in 1981 by the late President Brezhnev. Apparently the local intelligence community does not read Brezhnev's speeches; nevertheless, a community of even very low intelligence should ask itself a very simple question: Why are Soviet proposals—from the "verifiable freeze" to the "no-first-use" of nuclear weapons and the "demilitarization of outer space"—always taken up by Western "peace movements," while those forwarded by American and West European governments are ignored and very often derided?

Most importantly, the Soviets do not even attempt to conceal the fact that they manipulate the "peace movements" in Western Europe. Indeed, they openly admit that they have given them financial assistance. Thus, in the February 1982 issue of an official Novosti Press Agency magazine, *Sputnik* (published in English, French, German, and Russian, and available in the bookshops of these countries), there appeared an editorial that explained, with remarkable frankness, precisely what the purpose of the Soviet Peace Fund was: to give financial support to organizations, movements, and individuals who "struggle for peace and disarmament," and to sponsor international congresses, symposia, festivals, and exhibitions to give these organizations and individuals the opportunity to coordinate their activities on an international scale.

Later, on April 30, 1982, an article in *Pravda*, written by the head of the official Soviet Peace Committee, Yuri Zhukov (who is also a member of the CPSU's Central Committee), reported that the Soviet people enthusiastically contribute to the Soviet Peace Fund. According to Zhukov, over 80 million Soviet people had already made such contributions. Moreover, on May 31, 1982, *Pravda* reported that as of that date the Soviet people were obliged to donate one day's wages to the Soviet Peace Fund. The sum of money raised in this manner would be astronomical: the average one-day earnings of a Soviet worker is five rubles; multiplying this by the number of "donors" indicated by Zhukov—80 million—means that 400,000,000 rubles would be available to the Soviet Peace Fund.

Clearly, some of the money is used inside the Soviet Union, as Yuri Zhukov informs us, to support 120 regional peace committees across the country. Still, if we were to assume that each regional committee employed, say, a maximum of twenty full-time employees (there are nineteen employees at the headquarters of the Campaign for Nuclear Disarmament in Britain), we would have only a total of 2,400 full-time workers for the entire organization inside the Soviet Union. Multiplied by the annual earnings of the average Soviet worker, 2,000 rubles, this would amount to less than five million rubles as the total amount of money spent on wages by the Soviet Peace Fund inside the Soviet Union. Even if the expenses for travel, telephones, stationery, rents, and utilities were added to this amount, it would certainly not exceed 10 million rubles.

Let us suppose, then, that the Soviet Peace Fund sponsors trips for about 50,000 Western visitors to the Soviet Union per year. Let us also suppose that they receive royal treatment, the cost of which would unlikely be more than 5,000 rubles per trip. Even such an extremely generous estimate would account for only 250 million rubles. Adding the 10 million rubles which support the committees inside the Soviet Union gives us a total of 260 million rubles as a rough estimate of the accountable expenditures of the Soviet Peace Fund. Therefore, even if we were to compute a figure based on a minimum rate of donations and a maximum amount of expenses for internal activities, we would still be left with 140 million rubles to spend outside the Soviet Union, money to be used for sponsoring international conferences, festivals and exhibitions, and for supporting the activities of peace movements in the West. Even if this amount were converted into dollars using a "black market" rate of exchange, the Soviets would have available some $35–$45 million. The official rate of exchange would bring about $233 million.

WESTERN SLEEPWALKERS

Finally, confirmation of the Soviet manipulation of the peace movement came from the leader of the European Nuclear Disarmament (END) organization himself, Professor E. P. Thompson. In a remarkable article, Thompson criticized his colleagues in the peace movement, calling them "sleepwalkers" who either do not see or refuse to worry about Soviet strategy toward the peace movement in the West.[12] As Thompson asserts: "The sleepwalkers in the peace movement can see no problem in all this.

The United States intervenes continually in the West European political scene, and it is all a novelty to see the Soviet Union doing the same with success. And certain immediate Soviet aims run in the same direction as the aims of the peace movement. After all, they are quite as much against cruise missiles as is the most dedicated Western activist." He continues: ". . .alongside the Soviet peace offensive, clumsy attempts are now being made to split the Western peace movement and to bring it in line with Soviet strategies. There is now a busy traffic of meddlesome peace brokers between East and West, mini-conferences (summoned by selective invitation) in Moscow, and preparations for a huge show-case 'Peace Assembly' in Prague."[13]

In another article, E. P. Thompson writes:

> We do not stand in particular need of lessons from Yuri Zhukov, the President of the Soviet Peace Committee. Yet we have been receiving from him, and from several other sources in the Soviet Union and Eastern Europe, rather a lot of instructions in the past few months. . . . And Zhukov and his friends in the World Peace Council are trying in an old-fashioned 1950ish way to split our movement and bring it under the Soviet hegemony.
>
> To the Russians, we are background music only, and music not even loud enough to swing a German election.
>
> Our problems have been made worse in recent months by inept Soviet interventions in Western political life (including the peace movements). . . .
>
> We are willing to engage in discussions with official organizations over there, provided that the discussion is on honest and equal terms, and not on terms which coopt us into some pro-Soviet theatre of propaganda.[14]

WHAT HAS CHANGED IN THE PEACE MOVEMENT?

Clearly, these quotations from E. P. Thompson's articles indicate a sense of crisis in the West European "peace movement." This feeling of crisis and even possible split is further increased by the reports about the resignation of the most prominent figure in the German Green Party, former General Gert Bastian, caused by the seizure of key party positions by members of the Marxist-Leninist Communist League. According to the *New York Times* report (February 10, 1984), Bastian said that situation has undercut the Greens' commitment to non-violence and an even-handed stand between NATO and the Warsaw Pact by generating "a strong anti-American undertow." What has happened?

For one thing, a constant stream of criticism of the pro-Soviet orientation of peace movement propaganda has forced many anti-nuclear activists to become more critical of the Soviet Union. Peace movement leaders have not, for example, been able to continue their normal practice of excluding Soviet SS-20s from their usual condemnation of nuclear weapons. Nor have they been able to remain silent about Poland and Afghanistan.

At first, this criticism of Soviet policies and the SS-20s was tolerated by Moscow. As Soviet Peace Committee head Yuri Zhukov said, "What is our motto? No nuclear weapons in Europe—in East and West. No to nuclear weapons all over the world. We say we are against American missiles, Soviet missiles, French missiles, British missiles, and Chinese missiles. The bourgeois press totally conceals it."[15]

Later, however, as criticism of the Soviet position increased in Western peace movements, the Soviets began to lose patience with the more impartial position taken by moderates. It became too dangerous. Thus, the peace movement may face the possibility of splitting between more pro-Soviet elements and more impartial ones.

As E. P. Thompson wrote in June 1983, "On one side, Yuri Zhukov and the operators of the World Peace Council accuse some of us of being 'anti-Soviet elements'; on the other side Michael Heseltine and Monsignor Bruno Heim accuse some of us of being 'useful idiots' and apologists for Soviet aggression."[16]

The first blow came with the imposition of martial law in Poland. As Thompson insists, quite correctly, "the unprecedented demonstrations [totaled] more than two million people in Western European capitals in October and November 1981. And why were there not three million or four million demonstrating in the spring and summer of 1982? The answer is martial law in Poland and the repression of Solidarity."[17]

The second blow came from the Soviet position itself—the Soviet refusal to dismantle some of their SS-20s as a first step toward nuclear disarmament. The American "zero-option" proposal, the negotiations in Geneva, the more energetic propaganda of people committed to *multilateral* disarmament—all these developments have toned down the blatantly pro-Soviet position of many peace activists.

But the most devastating blow came with the persecution of the independent peace movements in Eastern Europe, primarily in East Germany and the Soviet Union. As twenty leaders of the American peace movement asserted in their letter to Brezhnev in September 1982:

The double standards by which the Soviet government abides—applauding widespread debate in the West, while crushing the most benign form of free expression at home—only strengthens the complex of forces that impel the nuclear arms race.

Renewed repression in the East, in particular of independent peace voices, will weaken Western peace movements and could—if they do not take precautions—paint them into an ineffectual 'pro-Soviet' corner.[18]

In a similar vein, Thompson has asked:

But what can we do about it? To refuse to go to the conference [in Prague] might be seen as a refusal to "talk with the other side," which everyone now wants to do. To go might be seen as condoning the Soviet occupation of Czechoslovakia. . .as well as an acceptance of the repression of civil rights workers who have been trying to open a dialogue with the Western peace movement. *This question puts us at sixes and sevens and divides us more than any propaganda by President Reagan could do.*[19]

Despite these reservations, the European "peace movement" decided to send representatives to Prague, knowing full well that, according to Thompson, "the media in the West will expose us all, without discrimination, as Soviet stooges," and that "the event will do only harm to the cause of peace and will alienate democrats in the East from Western peace forces." He went on to say:

The principle of solidarity with unofficial and independent peace voices on the other side was endorsed by the majority of the multitude of peace organizations from Europe and the United States attending the Second European Nuclear Disarmament Convention in West Berlin last month [May]. Sadly, the official "peace committees" of the East boycotted the convention, while our independent friends in East Germany, Hungary, the Soviet Union, and Czechoslovakia were refused exist visas to attend.[20]

Meanwhile, personal contacts between Western peace movement activists and leaders of the independent peace groups in the Eastern bloc were developed. Now, when taking their pilgrimage to Moscow, the Western peace movers have little excuse not to visit their counterparts. They inevitably witness the KGB persecution and the generally oppressive nature of the Soviet regime, and they slowly learn what I tried to explain to them two years ago in my pamphlet: that the internal oppressiveness and external aggressiveness of the Soviet regime are inseparable. They have suddenly learned that, as Thompson asserts, "Those weeping grandmothers, who still deck with flowers the graves of the last war, have dry eyes for Afghanistan, as they had, in 1968, for Czechoslovakia. The Soviet people will support their rulers in preparations for any war which is 'in defense of peace.'"[21] Finally, repeating almost word for word what I had written two years before, he states that "It is nonsense to try to extract something called 'the nuclear arms race' from the ideological and political context of which it is an integral part."[22]

PROBLEMS FOR THE SOVIETS

The women who occupied Greenham Commons may still be a nuisance to the British government, but they have also become a problem for the Soviets. During their visit to Moscow in May 1983, they brought a member of an unofficial Russian peace group to an official meeting of the Soviet government's peace committee, thereby forcing Soviet officials to listen to a Russian dissident in an official forum.[23] Defending the arrested members of the Moscow independent peace group, the Greenham Commons women chided their hosts: "It is as easy to sit down in front of the Soviet Embassy as at the Greenham Commons."[24]

Clearly, the day when peace activists in the West refuse to march in demonstrations with Communists, when this Soviet-inspired alliance is terminated, and when the crowds in European capitals demand the liberation of arrested peace activists in East Germany, the Soviet Union, Hungary, and Czechoslovakia as vigorously as they protest against nuclear weapons—that will be the day when the Soviets' political weapon of "peace" will turn against them.

Obviously, the Soviets realize the danger of losing control over the Western "peace movement." But what can they do? Expel all independent peace activists from the Soviet Union? If that were to happen, hundreds of thousands of Russians seeking an exit visa might then join the unofficial peace movement. Perhaps they will try to split the peace movement in the West, as Thompson believes they are now trying to do. But who knows how many peace activists would remain to support Moscow's policies—apart from Communist comrades?

One thing is clear: Soviet leaders cannot allow an independent peace movement to flourish in the Soviet Union, or in any of the satellites either, for they simply cannot tolerate the existence of any politically independent movement within their borders. Now that their troops are in Afghanistan, this is even more true.

Nor can the Soviet Union allow the Western "peace movements" to split up on its own, which is already happening in many countries. As a recent Moscow shortwave radio report indicated, this became a major Soviet concern and a reason for calling a special Conference of Representatives of Anti-War Movements of Europe and North America in Helsinki in October 1984:

> Special attention was given to a precise definition of the goals for the anti-war movement in its activity at the present stage. Many delegates, among them from the United States, Britain, Belgium, and France, all belonging to different political trends, unanimously noted that the enemies of peace have devised sophisticated methods of undermining the anti-war movement, in a bid to force them off the course of the anti-nuclear struggle, and push some of them onto the road of revising the existing frontiers in Europe and meddling in the Socialist countries' internal affairs. Speakers at the conference exposed and denounced the maneuvers of those who seek to disunite the anti-war movement by dividing them into the so-called Western and Eastern groups. . . . [25]

THE WESTERN POSITION

How well do Western politicians understand these new developments? Or, more precisely, how well do they understand that the questions of the arms race and disarmament do not exist outside the broader context of East-West relations? Do they understand that we are dealing with an ideological war that has very little to do with military hardware per se?

Judging by their behavior in the "nuclear debate," I would say that they do not understand it very well. Even leaving aside such questionable political actions as the recent Congressional approval of the nuclear freeze resolution [1983], the current policy of the Western alliance in the nuclear debate is pathetic. It all consists of passive reactions to Soviet moves, proposals, and rhetorical exercises.

Of course, there were a few successes, such as President Reagan's "zero option" proposal, and a brilliant resolution passed by the United Nations in December 1982 protecting the right of individuals to organize peace movements.

But these timid steps in the right direction were never developed into a clear strategy for the West, although the need for, and the direction of, such a strategy were quite obvious. Once a mass political movement has come into being in a democratic country and is well-organized and well-financed, one cannot easily eliminate it. Nor should the legitimate concern of its supporters to avoid nuclear destruction be perceived as necessarily hostile to democracy. Indeed, a concerted effort should be made to prevent the manipulation of such a movement by a foreign power. A strategy should be devised to counter Soviet efforts to penetrate and dominate Western peace movements.

As the Soviets try to unite everyone behind their "peace" drives, our effort should be aimed at thwarting them by emphasizing the most controversial aspects of their campaign. Persecution of independent peace groups in Communist countries and persistent Soviet violations of previous agreements should become targets of our counterattack. All confirmed facts of direct Soviet involvement with the peace movement in the West should be widely publicized. And, while the Soviets use the trick of the "absolute value," the "relative" horrors of Communist rule should become a centerpiece of Western counterpropaganda, focusing on such graphic events as Soviet atrocities in Afghanistan, mass murder in Cambodia, and famine in Ethiopia. While the Soviets channel their funds through their most loyal groups within the peace movement, ways should be found to support more moderate groups.

But, most importantly, the issues of peace and the arms race should be returned to the natural context of East-West relations, with public attention being constantly redirected to Soviet intentions instead of the sheer amount of weapons accumulated by both sides. Paradoxically, the best Western position was formulated long before the peace movement became an issue. It is the Helsinki Accords, signed in 1975 by thirty-five countries of Europe, Canada and the United States, which links respect for human rights with the problems of security. All the West needed to counter the Soviet "peace" campaign of the past four years was to return to this formula, conveniently endorsed by the signature of Brezhnev and other East European rulers. The logic of this position is impeccable: How can we control the arms race without verification, and how can we achieve verification without mutual trust? For that matter, how can anyone trust a government that does not allow its people to know the truth and discuss it and that deliberately instills hostility and hatred toward other nations into the minds of its population? How can we build trust with a nation whose citizens are not allowed to have a sincere and open dialogue with foreigners, under threat of imprisonment? As Andrei Sakharov, the only Russian ever to receive the Nobel Peace Prize, writes: "As long as a country has no civil liberty, no freedom of information, and no independent press, then there exists no effective body of public opinion to control the conduct of government. Meanwhile, the [Soviet] military-industrial complex and the KGB are gaining in strength, threatening the stability of the entire world, and super-militarization is eating up all our resources." "A most important concept, which in time became a cornerstone of my position," writes Sakharov in his letter to Anatoly Alexandrov, president of the USSR Academy of Sciences, "is the indissoluble bond between international security and trust on the one hand, and respect for human rights and an open society on the other."

Ironically, this clear position could easily become a basis for the long-coveted bi-partisan foreign policy in America, if any administration ever tried to offer it. In his Special Appeal for Peace Day, Governor Mario Cuomo, who can hardly be described as a conservative hardliner, states:

> The risk of nuclear war between the United States and the Soviet Union can be reduced if all people can express their opinions freely and without fear on domestic and world issues, including their nation's arms policies.
> The Soviet Union is a signatory of the Universal Declaration of Human Rights of the United Nations as signed thirty-six years ago. The Soviet Union is also a signatory of the Helsinki Agreements, which promise the facilitation of travel, uninhibited exchange of information, reunification of families, review of applications for visas, and the right of all people to enjoy personal and religious freedom.
> International tension will be lessened and international stability enhanced through complete acceptance and implementation of the Universal Declaration of Human Rights of the United Nations and the Helsinki Agreements by all signatories.

Earlier, on October 25, 1984, the Massachusetts House of Representatives, which is not known to be dominated by conservative stalwarts, adopted a *Resolution Urging the Soviet Union to Abide by the Universal Declaration of Human Rights of the United Nations and the Helsinki Agreements as a Means toward Reducing the Threat of Nuclear War.*

Those who may doubt the possible success of using this approach will be interested to know the idea was tested in Los Angeles on June 5, 1984, when the voters were offered the following proposition:

> Shall the Los Angeles County Board of Supervisors transmit to the leaders of the United States and the Soviet Union a communication stating that the risk of nuclear war between the United States and the Soviet Union can be reduced if all people have the ability to express their opinions freely and without fear on world issues including the nations' arms

policies; therefore, the people of Los Angeles County urge all nations that signed the Helsinki Accords on Human Rights to observe the Accords' provisions on freedom of speech, religion, press, assembly, and emigration for all their citizens?

Despite vehement opposition by leaders of the nuclear freeze movement, the measure was carried by nearly a two-thirds majority.[26] Unfortunately, this idea has never been used on a national scale, let alone in the international arena.

MISTAKEN PREMISES OF NEGOTIATIONS

Instead, U.S. leaders decided to begin arms reduction negotiations in Geneva—a big mistake, in my view. First of all, the idea of dragging the West into negotiations belongs to the Soviet strategists and represents a considerable victory for them. (See the resolution of the Soviet-sponsored World Parliament of Peoples for Peace, which, among other things, contains the demand: "Negotiate! There is no choice!"[27]) It is not difficult to understand why the Soviets badly needed to bring the United States into arms control negotiations: (a) they had been placed in political isolation by the invasion of Afghanistan, a plight that would be mitigated by arms negotiations; (b) SALT II had been rejected by the Senate; and (c) the West had finally awakened to discover that the Soviets had achieved strategic superiority, and Western leaders were about to engage in a new arms buildup.

Why did the West accept the Soviet call for arms control negotiations? It was clearly against Western interests because (a) it is always bad to accept the idea of the enemy; and (b) even worse to do so under the pressure of the Soviet-inspired peace movement; and (c) arms negotiations with the Soviets are de facto justification of two major Soviet propaganda themes: that the danger of nuclear war is greater now than ever before (a position that works against Western efforts to match the Soviet arms buildup), and that the Western doctrine of nuclear deterrence does not work (and therefore does not need to be shored up by adding more nuclear weapons); (d) it is not wise to negotiate from a position of inferiority, as the West would be doing until its arms buildup was well along; (e) negotiations have reinforced the Soviet effort to focus the world's attention on the nuclear problem and away from Soviet aggression in Afghanistan and elsewhere; and (f) it amounted to acceptance of the dubious notion that it is possible to have mutually advantageous agreements with the Soviet Union, and that the Kremlin can be relied upon to abide by international agreements—despite the evidence on record, for example, the Helsinki Accords.

But more importantly, entering into arms negotiations with the Soviet Union means that the West has essentially accepted the Soviet proposition that the main threat in the world today comes from bombs and missiles and not from the Soviet system itself. In other words, it has amounted to an acceptance of the notion that disarmament can be discussed outside the context of East-West relations.

All in all, it was an unbelievably inconsistent and irresponsible political decision. As a result, the United States has appeared to be weak, frightened, and under constant pressure. Once again, the Soviets have scored a propaganda victory and forced the West into a defensive position, and they did this at a time when they were vulnerable—at a time when they had been caught cheating on arms control agreements and the Helsinki Accords, and, above all, after having committed outright aggression in Afghanistan.

One can hardly perceive as an American victory the fact that the Soviets, overestimating their influence on world public opinion, did not force the West into further concessions when they walked out of the Geneva talks and deliberately increased international tensions. American foreign policy has become hostage to the idea of an inevitable arms control process, while tired Western societies are quite ready to return to the Soviet version of détente. It is a safe prediction that the Soviets will be more successful at the next stage of this vicious cycle.

Still worse, retreating further from what could be its position of advantage, the West seems to have accepted another Soviet idea and agreed to discuss "trust-building measures" with the Soviet Union separately from the issue of human rights. The Stockholm conference is probably the most vivid example of how little Western politicians understand about the nature of the problem they confront. I wonder what they discuss with the Soviets behind those closed doors in Stockholm: trust-building measures that are secret from the entire world but not from the Soviets? When the Helsinki Accords are so easily forgotten (without being officially repealed), who can trust any new treaty that may be concluded?

Instead of START (Strategic Arms Reduction Talks) or INF (Intermediate Nuclear Forces) talks, the West should propose convening a conference to negotiate a postwar peace treaty in Europe, which to this day does not exist. Such a conference would allow us to concentrate on the real issues and the real threat to Western Europe and the United States, namely, the Soviet empire. Clearly, negotiating a peace treaty in Europe would be impossible without discussing Soviet postwar acquisitions and the occupation of Eastern Europe, without repealing the Hitler-Stalin Pact, and without discussing the unification of Germany and the withdrawal of foreign troops from European countries. This move would generate enormous pressure on the Soviets and force *them* onto the defensive.

Ideologically, the Soviet position would be untenable. They would not be able credibly to deny a referendum to countries occupied as a result of the Hitler-Stalin Pact, while at the same time posing as a champion of European peace. In addition, focusing public attention on an all-European peace conference would most likely generate unrest in the already explosive areas of the Baltic states and the Western Ukraine. It would touch on the Soviet Union's most painful problem: the problem of nationalities.

Paradoxically, in such a conference the Soviet bloc would not be as monolithic as might be expected. Most of the East and Central European countries have numerous territorial claims on the Soviet Union and on each other, and the nationalistic feelings of all East Europeans would inevitably be stirred.

Given the current climate of peace hysteria, the Soviets could hardly refuse to participate in such a conference. Should they, nevertheless, refuse to attend, the burden of blame for the arms race, international tension, and the danger of nuclear holocaust would shift to the Kremlin, the crowds would move to our side, and Soviet influence over the Western peace movements would be lost.

CONCLUSION

Within a few years very little will be left of the "peace movement" in Europe. As soon as the new missiles are safely stationed, the current wave of aggressive pacifism will begin to subside. Most of these marchers will return to their usual pastimes: television, football, and the like. And nothing will penetrate their apathy.

Perhaps I will be the only one who will feel sorry because of it. For the first time in thirty years, the Soviets have handed us a powerful weapon which could have been turned against them to reverse the existing trend in international relations and neutralize the present source of danger in the world. Yet through our lack of understanding and wisdom, we have failed to grasp the opportunity.

Thus, it seems that we will continue to squander billions of dollars in an endless arms race. We will continue to fight Communism on the outskirts of our countries, but each time closer and closer to our homes. We will continue to deceive ourselves with the expectations that a "closet liberal" will somehow manage to make his way to the top of the Soviet ruling circles, or that the Communist dictatorship will somehow be overthrown by a military coup. We will continue "business as usual" with Moscow—and naively hope for the best.

FOOTNOTES

1. Vladimir Bukovsky, *The Peace Movement and the Soviet Union*, (New York: Orwell Press, 1982); "Better Red than Dead is not Good Enough," *Times* (London), December 4, 1981; "The Peace Movement and the Soviet Union," *Commentary*, May 1982. See, also, *Les Pacifistes contre la Paix* (Paris: Edition Robert Laffont, 1982); and *Pazifisten gegen den Frieden* (Bern, Switzerland: Verlag SOI, 1983). This pamphlet was also published in Sweden, the Netherlands, Denmark, Norway, Greece, and Turkey, and reprinted in two collections of papers in the United States.

2. *Pravda*, September 23-29, 1980; *Izvestia*, September 23-24, 27-28, 1980.

3. *Los Angeles Times*, May 11, 1983.

4. *Washington Post*, May 11, 1983.

5. *The New Yorker*, September 3, 1984.

6. *Ibid.*

7. *Ibid.*

8. The internal developments of the Labor Party are typical for any left-of-center political organization, especially in Europe (including the German Social Democratic party): they are usually taken over by the left radicals and Communists from within, unless they undergo a split. The scandals over the Communist infiltration into the British Labor Party continued for several years, until the moderate part split off and formed the Social Democratic Party a few years ago. The Labor Party in Britain today is greatly influenced by its Communist elements, and its 1984 platform includes unilateral nuclear disarmament, withdrawal from NATO, and a number of East European-type economic reforms.

9. *Wall Street Journal*, February 22, 1983.

10. Lord Chalfont, "The Great Unilateral Illusion," *Encounter*, April 1983; and Wynfred Joshua, "Soviet Manipulation of the European Peace Movement," *Strategic Review*, Winter 1983.

11. See John Vinocur, "West European Foes of New U.S. Missiles Often Find KGB Men in Their Midst," *New York Times*, July 26, 1983; Associated Press Dispatch, April 29, 1983; and John Barron; "The KGB's Magical War for Peace," *Reader's Digest*, October 1982.

12. *Guardian*, February 21, 1983.

13. *Ibid.*

14. E. P. Thompson, "Peace and the East," *New Society*, June 2, 1983, pp. 349-352.

15. *Guardian*, April 14, 1983.

16. Thompson, *op. cit.*

17. *Ibid.*

18. *Ibid.*

19. *Ibid.*

20. *Ibid.*

21. *Guardian*, February 21, 1983.

22. *Ibid.*

23. *Times*, (London) May 27, 1983.

24. *Ibid.*

25. Radio Moscow report by special correspondent Alexander Pagadin from Helsinki, Radio Moscow, North American Service (shortwave), October 8, 1984: 4:20, 8:20, 9:20, and 11:20 p.m.

26. *Wall Street Journal*, June 11, 1984, p. 22; and *The Washington Times*, June 8, 1984.

27. *Pravda*, September 26, 1980.

Enduring Misconceptions about the Soviet Union

PAUL HOLLANDER

LEARNING ABOUT THE SOVIET SYSTEM has never been easy. The language barrier, a secretive regime, lack of opportunity for field studies, and limited scholarly contacts have all combined to limit the flow of information. Even today, only a handful of social scientists specialize in Soviet studies or teach courses about Soviet society. Over the years, I have come to realize, however, that the problem has not been the lack of information as such, and under Khrushchev and Brezhnev it even became easier to learn about certain aspects of Soviet society, with Soviet social scientists and journalists contributing to the growth of knowledge and providing occasional revelations that had formerly been proscribed.

Numerous authentic accounts of Soviet concentration camps had been published in the West before Solzhenitsyn's Gulag series, though they received little attention. There was likewise information about the less genial aspects of Stalin's personality before Khrushchev addressed himself to the topic at the Twentieth Party Congress. Public awareness of such matters, however, remained negligible. Curiously enough, even before anti-Communism had the unsavory reputation (in liberal circles, at any rate) it later acquired as a consequence of the activities of the late Senator Joseph McCarthy, a thorough understanding of the Soviet system was a rare phenomenon. Anti-Communists, moreover, were no better informed than the sympathizers or those otherwise inclined to give Soviet authorities the benefit of the doubt.

I have gradually come to realize that it is not information about the actual state of affairs in Soviet society—published in scholarly journals by well-funded researchers with the requisite language skills—that determines

PAUL HOLLANDER is a professor of sociology at the University of Massachusetts (Amherst) and is best known for his *Political Pilgrims: Travels of Western Intellectuals to the Soviet Union, China, and Cuba.* His essay first appeared in *The World & I*, October 1986, and is reprinted with permission.

U.S. beliefs about and attitudes toward the Soviet Union. They are determined rather by domestic political and cultural conditions and by "climates of opinion."

American and Western misconceptions of the Soviet Union have a long and remarkable history — as long as that of the Soviet Union itself. I have documented and analyzed many of these misconceptions in a study entitled *Political Pilgrims*.

WISHFUL THINKING

Except for Billy Graham's praise for Soviet religious freedom and for the caviar generously provided for distinguished visiting dignitaries like himself, nothing today quite matches the bizarre misconceptions and grotesque misperceptions common in the 1930s and early 1940s among some of the most revered intellectuals and public figures of the times. These included such writers, philosophers, scientists, and journalists as Louis Aragon, Henri Barbusse, J.D. Bernal, Bertolt Brecht, Malcolm Cowley, John Dewey, Theodore Dreiser, W.E.B. DuBois, Lion Feuchtwanger, Louis Fisher, Julian Huxley, Harold Laski, Pablo Neruda, Romain Rolland, Jean-Paul Sartre, G.B. Shaw, Upton Sinclair, Anna Louise Strong, H.G. Wells, Edmund Wilson, and many others.

It is significant that admiration for the Soviet Union peaked between the late 1920s and the mid-1930s — that is, during the period of the forced collectivization of agriculture and the attendant famines, the Purge, the establishment of the cult of Stalin, and the Moscow trials. This suggests that the actual nature of a political system and its evaluation by outsiders may be entirely independent of each other. Generations of Western visitors — especially during the 1930s — managed to tour the USSR and see nothing but the fairyland carefully fabricated by their hosts to shield them from unpleasant impressions and experiences.

Western intellectuals who visited the Soviet Union in the 1930s were characterized by an overwhelmingly favorable predisposition to project upon the Soviet Union their hopes and expectations. They were particularly impressed by the sense of purpose and community they discovered, the sense of justice and social equality, the dedication and sincerity of the leaders, the spirit of popular participation, the rise of the New Soviet Man, and the humaneness of the political system, including its enlightened penal policies.

That such erroneous beliefs and misperceptions could exist suggests that predisposition predetermines perception and that conditions in Western societies generated expectations for which fulfillment was sought elsewhere. American intellectuals and opinion leaders thus flocked to the Soviet Union in the 1920s and 1930s looking for alternatives to the economic and social bankruptcy of the Depression years. The Soviet Union with its planned economy, full employment, and (specious) political stability presented an appealing antithesis to the crisis-ridden societies of the West.

A Recurring Phenomenon

That phenomenon recurred in the 1960s, 1970s, and 1980s. In the 1960s, the attention of American intellectuals was drawn to Cuba, a new revolutionary society of great apparent vitality that presented striking contrast to the racial problems, social injustice, and empty affluence the critics deplored in the United States. Involvement in the Vietnam War intensified the quest for more just and peaceful societies, which some believed they had found in Cuba, North Vietnam, or Mao's China. Sympathy for yet another Marxist-Leninist society sprang up in the 1980s when the actions and policies of the Reagan presidency gave rise to a new wave of social criticism and political estrangement that found emotionally satisfying expression in championing Nicaragua, which was seen as a victim of the Reagan administration and earlier American policy. In each instance, the idealization and misperception of Marxist-Leninist societies were conditioned by domestic discontents.

Among the recurring misconceptions is the belief that the Soviet system, stimulated by vigorous trade with the United States, is on the verge of recognizing the advantages of the free enterprise system and embracing the benefits of capitalistic methods of production and distribution. By doing so, Soviet leaders would thus gracefully preside over the gradual transformation and humanization of their system, and new capitalistic techniques would effect liberalization within both the cultural and political realms.

The readiness to attribute such propensities to Soviet leaders – besides being a manifestation of wishful thinking, a major and most enduring influence on American attitudes toward the Soviet Union derives from a pragmatic disposition that is reluctant to believe that political leaders can take ideas and ideologies seriously. The English author, Claude Cockburn, commented on these attitudes as early as the late 1920s: "Wall Street men . . . looked upon the USSR . . . as in effect just another fast-developing area with a big trade potential . . . as though the Revolution and the doctrines of Marxism-Leninism were puerile incidents, temporary deviations from the ultimate forward movement of the world alongside businesslike American lines."[1] William Barrett, in turn, observed in 1946 that "the fellow travelers. . .would love to believe that Russia is capitalist at heart, and so no worse, and therefore just as good—by God!—as anybody else."[2] More recently, Joseph Finder paraphrased a current version of this outlook: "[A] taste of capitalism would turn the old men of the Politburo from increasing military stockpiles to improving the Russian way of life."[3]

Of late, the plea for more trade and the desire for more profit have acquired an uplifting moral justification—namely, that trade will not only be profitable but assure lasting peace. As Donald M. Kendall of the Pepsi Corporation put it, "We should give the Soviet Union a stake in peace, which we are best prepared to give through trade."[4]

Generations of American business leaders such as Cyrus Eaton, Armand Hammer, Averell Harriman, and David Rockefeller entertained such ideas, finding it genuinely difficult to believe that Soviet leaders' calculations of cost-benefit ratios could be significantly different from their own or from those of any self-respecting head of a major business corporation. Efforts to assimilate the image of the Soviet Union to that of a modern business corporation have also been assisted by occasional scholarly efforts—for example, Alfred G. Meyer's conception of "USSR Incorporated"—that focus on the allegedly universal characteristics of modern bureaucratic organizations, which transcend political and ideological boundaries.

THE FEAR FACTOR

Probably the major source of such misconceptions of the Soviet system and the conduct and aspiration of its leaders is to be found in the related processes of projection and wishful thinking. They have been with us for a long time but have of late been given new impetus by the fear of nuclear war. Wishful thinking regarding Soviet foreign policy typically manifests itself in minimizing Soviet aggression when it occurs and in questioning any aggressive intent when it can be inferred from ideology or policy statements. The wishful observer accepts Soviet statements at their face value when they convey benevolent attitudes but disbelieves them when they reflect hostility or belligerence. In the latter case, they are viewed as mere rhetoric produced for domestic consumption, or dismissed as ideological window dressing, issued to please a few aged diehards or hawks left over from the days of Stalin. The combination of pragmatic and wishful thinking enables many Americans to play down simultaneously both the Soviet expressions of hostility and its ideological underpinnings.

It is not hard to understand why so many American businessmen, journalists, politicians, and peace activists have been disposed to deny or belittle the ideological foundations and determinants of Soviet attitudes and policies. If they were taken seriously, they would render Soviet expansionism more plausible and more highly patterned—the very phenomenon these groups prefer to ignore. The more seriously Soviet leaders take their ideology, the less likely will they be to accommodate the West, to behave like heads of just another status quo power, and to put domestic shortages ahead of foreign policy objectives. Crediting them with serious ideological commitments also clashes with the image of a team of pragmatic, technocratic, managerial types that wishful Americans have favored for decades. Even a perception of the Soviet Union as merely obeying the imperatives and dynamics of great-power status and filling the vacuum left by the other great powers is more comforting than the image of a political system propelled by a messianic urge to spread the true belief and export institutions that support it. When, therefore, Soviet expansionism is reluctantly acknowledged, it tends to be viewed by wishful thinkers as limited in its objectives, capable of satisfaction or appeasement, and a mere continuation of the age-old Russian quest for security.

Wishful thinking comes into play on those occasions when Soviet conduct is particularly painful to contemplate and when its realistic interpretation tends to undermine the observer's sense of security. Thus Vladimir Bukovsky, the Soviet dissident, observed:

> Even the most undeniable facts—like the shooting down of the Korean airliner. . .or the invasion of Afghanistan—failed to change public opinion in the West. Instead. . .Soviet behavior in both cases has prompted many to look for a more "rational" explanation of Soviet motives. . .And more often than not, these explanations tend to blame the Western governments rather than the Soviets.
>
> In general, whenever a person is confronted with something mindboggling. . .horrible and beyond his control, he goes through a succession of mental states ranging from denial to guilt, from fantastic rationalizations to acute depression.[5]

Wishful thinking often appears in conjunction with efforts to "understand" Soviet behavior. Long before the earnest present-day appeals to goodwill and understanding on behalf of peace and friendship, William Barrett had spotted and criticized this attitude as early as 1946. To the advice that "we must be neither for nor against Russia, but we must try to understand her," Barrett responded: "Analogously, we should have been neither for nor against Hitler, but simply have tried to understand him."

THE THERAPEUTIC APPROACH

Barrett's comment is a reminder that appeals to "understand" and thereby regard with a measure of sympathy the behavior of either individuals or political entities are always made selectively. Just as few pleaded for sympathetically understanding the Nazis, so today few would argue for sympathetically understanding the Afrikaners and their abhorrent policies of segregation and discrimination. The obvious reason such arguments are not made is that doing so would blunt the edge of moral indignation toward South African whites. By way of contrast, appeals for understanding the Soviet leaders and their policies have proliferated in the 1980s, giving rise to what I have called the therapeutic approach toward Soviet behavior. George F. Kennan, for example, wrote:

> [T]hese Soviet Communists with whom we will now have to deal are flesh-and-blood people like ourselves, misguided if you will but no more guilty than we are of the circumstances into which they were born. They too, like ourselves, are simply trying to make the best of it.[6]

Elsewhere Kennan lapsed into a clinical vocabulary in describing Soviet leaders and the reason they deserve understanding and sympathy. He saw them as having "a congenital sense of insecurity" and a "neurotic fear of penetration," as being "easily frightened," and further characterized them as frustrated, obsessive, secretive, defensive, fixated, troubled, and anxious. He also perceived them

> as a group of quite ordinary men [the "banality of evil" thesis of Hannah Arendt], to some extent victims...of the ideology on which they have been reared, but shaped far more importantly by the discipline of responsibilities...as rulers of a great country...more seriously concerned to preserve the present limits of their political power than to expand those limits...whose motivation is essentially defensive... whose attention is riveted primarily on the unsolved problems of economic development within their own country.[7]

Kennan and his followers have viewed the Soviet Union as being in the grip of necessity and without alternatives — constrained or propelled by a form of selective historical determinism that deprives it of sensible choices, though it allows great freedom of action to its adversaries. A historical destiny, it is claimed, compels the Soviet Union to act sometimes imprudently, to expand, to conquer (or at least not to relinquish conquests), to repress dissent at home, and to conduct itself generally in ways that Western observers view with regret and distaste, but, more importantly, with understanding and never judgmentally. Thus, for example, Jerry Hough advises against a "rush to judgment" of the Soviet invasion of Afghanistan and generally appreciates the influence of "feelings of anger and grievance on Soviet policy."[8]

REVISIONIST SCHOLARSHIP

This therapeutic approach is discernible in various degrees in the work of such scholars as Steven Cohen, Stanley Hoffman, Jerry Hough, Theodore von Laue, Marshall Shulman, and their younger colleagues of the "revisionist" school of Soviet historiography.

One major premise of this approach is the insistence that Western scholars and politicians not employ culturally conditioned Western criteria in their interpretation and evaluation of Soviet affairs. They must be aware, for instance, that what appears as aggressive behavior to us may be only the acting out of historically conditioned insecurities and apprehensions. In the therapeutic approach, unattractive forms of Soviet behavior—including abusive rhetoric and hostile propaganda—must not be protested overmuch but excused rather as due to a difficult past. Such tolerance will generate trust and promote better international and Soviet-American relations.

Some of the associated premises bolstering the therapeutic approach are: (1) the Soviet Union is a status quo power; (2) there is a basic symmetry between the superpowers; (3) many or most of the tensions between them result from mutually reinforcing misperceptions and misunderstandings; (4) anti-Soviet or anti-Communist attitudes are basically irrational; (5) the Cold War was the reflection for the most part of such attitudes rather than a genuine conflict of interests; and (6) when the relations between the superpowers are warmer and friendlier, Soviet domestic policies become more liberal. Such components and correlatives of the therapeutic approach have recently received increasing vocal expression and have been asssimilated into the ideology of the peace movement, which insists that only the kind of understanding sketched above will avert nuclear holocaust.

A culmination of the non-judgmental, therapeutic approach was the attempt by the historian Theodore von Laue to restore the image of Stalin morally and historically.

Laue's vision of Stalin is inseparable from the conception of Russia as the underdog and eternal victim, which required a Stalin as the tough-minded redeemer of his victimized nation. As is often the case, Laue's hesitancy at condemning Stalin or the Soviet Union is more than balanced by his animosity toward the United States and his indignation toward his more judgmental colleagues:

> American and Western historians have sat solemnly and self-righteously in judgment of Stalin. One wondered by what right, by what standards, by what power of their imagination? How can the bookish tribe of scholars judge the harsh realities which shaped Stalin and his judgment?. . .Our sights cleared at last, we are left to praise Stalin as a tragic giant set into the darkest part of the twentieth century. . . .
> Praise then to the strength and fortitude of mind and body that raised Stalin to such heights—and compassion too for his frailties.[9]

In other statements, Laue undertook to save us from the "guilt of moral imperialism." His reassessment of Stalin represents a bizarre culmination of a one-sided historical determinism that cast the Soviet Union once and for all in the role of an underdog nation and sought to explain or excuse every aspect of Soviet conduct as the outcome of the imperatives of modernization in the face of supposedly insuperable odds and obstacles. The halo earned in the course of this uphill struggle was viewed as also belonging to Stalin.

THERAPEUTIC APPEASEMENT

The therapeutic approach may give rise to therapeutic appeasement, which differs from ordinary appeasement by the circuitous justification that it is not based, as is more customary, on the overwhelming strength of the power to be appeased but on its weakness. This type of appeasement is more acceptable psychologically and politically than one that justifies appeasement on the basis of the adversary's superior strength, since the latter acknowledges one's own weakness or fear. When a policy of appeasement is predicated upon the weakness, insecurity, or folly of the other side, the appeaser thereby assumes a superior, mature, and rational role. Why fight over banana republics, tribal countries in Africa, sundry quagmires, remote unimportant places like Angola or Afghanistan? Let them have Grenada, Benin, or the Malagasy Republic if that will make them happy. Let them gratify the childish, irrational, grabby impulses bred by their historical insecurity. We understand it all!

Some of these attitudes are not limited to relations with the Soviet Union but are linked to what Irving Kristol called "the liberal theory of antisocial behavior" in international affairs. In his view, the State Department has for some time "implicitly subscribed to what Philip Rieff called the 'therapeutic ethic,' according to which undisciplined nations would be chided for their transgressions. . .and would thereby learn to behave in a 'proper' and 'socially responsible' way. Even the strategy of containment of the Soviet Union had this theory behind it." [10] While such a theory applies to the Soviets insofar as their transgressions are seen as a temporary course of conduct that can be outgrown, there has been less emphasis on chiding than on forbearance and understanding.

As was noted earlier, projection is another mechanism that − in conjunction with wishful thinking and the therapeutic understanding − creates a distorted image of the Soviet Union. It comes into play when Soviet policies, institutions, and leaders are cast into forms familiar to the American experience. They have their hard lines and we have ours; their military lobbies for a larger slice of the budget pie and so does ours; they have their self-perpetuating bureaucracies and so do we; their leaders are under pressure to satisfy a public that demands more consumer goods and has no stomach for military adventures, while Americans pressure their elected representatives to spend more on human welfare and less on arms; their leaders believe no more in their ideological pronouncements than American politicians making speeches on the stump; they are as interested in the balance of power and global peace as we are. We blundered into Vietnam; they were drawn into Afghanistan. Similar projections by our business tycoons attributed Western economic rationality to Soviet political leaders.

FAVORABLE IMPRESSIONS

The convergence of projection and wishful thinking is especially pronounced when a new Soviet leader emerges and is greeted with effusive expressions of hope and confident anticipation that he will behave like an American politician. As E.J. Epstein, a critic of such perceptions, puts it:

Andropov's accession to power. . .was accompanied by a corresponding ennoblement of his image. Suddenly he became in *The Wall Street Journal* "silver-haired and dapper." His stature, previously reported in *The*

Washington Post as an unimpressive "five feet eight inches," was abruptly elevated to "tall and urbane." *The Times* noted that Andropov "stood conspicuously taller than most" Soviet leaders and that "his spectacles, intense gaze, and donnish demeanor gave him the air of a scholar."

Soon there were reports that Andropov was a man of extraordinary accomplishment. . . . According to an article in *The Washington Post*, Andropov "is fond of cynical political jokes with an anti-regime twist. . . collects abstract art, likes jazz. . .swims, plays tennis, and wears clothes that are sharply tailored in West European style. . . ." *The Wall Street Journal* added that Andropov "likes Glenn Miller records, good Scotch whisky, Oriental rugs, and American books." To the list of his musical favorites *Time* added "Chubby Checker, Frank Sinatra, Peggy Lee and Bob Eberly" and. . .said that he enjoyed singing "hearty renditions of Russian songs" at after-theater parties. The *Christian Science Monitor* suggested that he has "tried his hand at writing verse. . .of a comic variety."

According to *The Washington Post* Yuri Andropov is "a perfect host."[11]

More recently, similarly excited expectations were generated by Gorbachev's rise to power—an even more suitable target for wishful projections, since he is younger than his predecessors and boasts a well-dressed wife.

Members of a recent U.S. congressional delegation to Moscow came away with highly favorable impressions of Gorbachev, whom they perceived (as virtually all his predecessors also had been) as a man "we can do business with."

Speaker of the House Thomas O'Neill was impressed "not only with his politician's informality but also with [his] solid grasp of the issues and of American politics." O'Neill found him "easy and gracious. He is like one of those New York corporation lawyers." Senator Paul S. Sarbanes, a Maryland Democrat, suggested that the way Mr. Gorbachev "makes his points, as a lawyer does in reasoned fashion," made the Americans wonder whether he could be argued into compromises. Silvio Conte, a Massachusetts Republican, thought that "he would be a good candidate for New York City. . .a sharp dresser. . .[a] smooth guy." Robert Byrd, Senate Minority Leader, noted that "He is a younger man, educated, clever, and trained as a lawyer." As Hedrick Smith summed it up, "Mr. Gorbachev's mixture of wit and argument and his informal manner left several senators feeling as if they had met an American-style politician in the Kremlin."[12]

Clearly, Americans are eager to see Soviet politics and politicians in a highly personalized manner, as counterparts of American politics and politicians and portrayed as American politics is portrayed by the American media. Emphasis on the personal characteristics of Soviet leaders helps to humanize and assimilate them into the familiar American political and cultural context, makes them less threatening, and diminishes the significance of their ideological convictions and political values.

It should be pointed out that such projections are not merely or invariably the products of wishful thinking. Projection is also encouraged by simple ignorance and becomes a device for filling in the gaps of one's knowledge of Soviet behavior, policies, or institutions. In the absence of information to the contrary, it is tempting to assume that people all over the world have social and political arrangements, beliefs, and values similar to one's own. This tendency is strengthened by what remains of the American belief in universal progress: that countries all over the world will gradually and naturally gravitate toward some kind of political democracy; that it is difficult to rule people against their will; that human nature is basically good and sooner or later finds expression; that material improvements and political liberalization go hand in hand as do universal education and demands for liberty. Some of these beliefs also find their way into the so-called convergence theory of modern industrial societies, which predicts the gradual liberalization of Soviet society. The hope that a new Soviet leader will be better than his predecessor may be linked to the American cultural belief that change is usually for the better.

Rehabilitating the Past

Benign images of the Soviet Union examined herein have their roots in genuine political change — such as that which followed Stalin's death — but also in wishful thinking. Some scholarly reflection favorable to the Soviet system has rejected the concept of totalitarianism, which had previously been used to characterize the Soviet Union. Several years ago, I wrote that the concept of

> totalitarianism...has come under heavy criticism both by those who have come to believe that it has *never* been a useful concept and by those who think that it has been rendered obsolete by social change in the Soviet Union. The applicability of pluralism to American society in turn has been questioned most forcefully by C. Wright Mills and his numerous followers. Note that the growing denial of pluralism in American society by one group of social scientists has been paralleled by an increasing imputation of pluralism to the Soviet Union by another group. Indeed the search for signs of pluralism (however feeble or minor) in the

Soviet Union has been just as determined and purposeful as the pursuit of data to prove its nonexistence in the United States! These two endeavors have been carried out by different groups of scholars, yet they spring from the same underlying "Zeitgeist," which prompts many American intellectuals to approach their own society in the most critical spirit and other societies fearful of being critical — increasingly haunted by the specter of self-righteousness.[13]

This state of affairs is still with us. In the 1980s, the desire to see evidences of pluralism in the Soviet Union persists as does scepticism about pluralism in American society. Jerry Hough, for example, stated that the Soviet leadership under Brezhnev "almost seems to have made the Soviet Union closer to the spirit of the pluralist model of American political science than is the United States." He also discerned that there existed in the USSR political participation as meaningful as that in the United States and an effort to create constitutional restraints within the Soviet leadership.[14] Hough's perception of political participation in the Soviet Union is colored by a reluctance to distinguish between pseudo-participation that is a ritualistic endorsement of high level decisions performed under duress and official pressure on the one hand, and participation that is voluntary and can influence the political process on the other.[15]

A new school of revisionist scholarship has arisen that seeks to redefine — sometimes retroactively — the character of the Soviet system. The main thrust of this revisionist historiography has aimed at minimizing centralized authoritarianism in Soviet social and political transformations. Peter Kenez commented on such endeavors as follows:

> In the writings of the revisionists there is no ambiguity. Denying the extraordinary nature and importance of state intervention in the life of society is at the very heart of their interpretation of the 1930s. . . . Stalinism disappears as a phenomenon. In their presentation the politics of the 1930s was humdrum politics: interest groups fought with one another; the government was simply responding either to public pressure or. . .circumstances, such as the bad harvest. . . .[T]he Soviet government was just like any other government operating in difficult circumstances. This view is utterly contrary to all available evidence.[16]

Arch J. Getty, in his book *The Origin of the Great Purges* (1985), has presented a revisionist account of the Purges — the most ambitious attempt to date to rehabilitate the Soviet system by removing the stains of the past from the present by denying or overlooking the past and its greatest moral outrage. Kenez comments:

The very title. . . leads one to expect an explanation for one of the blood-
iest terrors in history. It soon turns out, however, that for Getty the
purges meant above all a revision of party rolls. . . . He then proceeds to
devote far more space to the 1935 exchange of party cards than to mass
murder. He adds, rather disingenuously, that he will not discuss in detail
the bloody aspects of his story, for that has been done by others. . . . His
choice of subject matter reminds one of a historian who chooses to write
an account of a shoe factory operating in. . . Auschwitz. He uses many
documents and he does not falsify the material. He decides not to use all
available sources and dismisses the testimony of survivors as "biased."
Instead he concentrates on factory records. He discusses matters of
production, supply and marketing. . . . He does not notice the gas
chambers.[17]

The Post-Vietnam Era

In the 1960s and early 1970s, perceptions of the Soviet Union were conditioned by U.S. involvement in Vietnam. Those preoccupied with critiques
of American society were disinclined to dwell on flaws of its foreign critics
and adversaries, including the Soviet Union. In the 1980s, other influences
have come into play. At every level of American society—from grass-roots
nuclear-freeze activists and promoters of sister cities and nuclear-free
zones to members of Congress and State Department officials—the specter
of nuclear war has become a determinant of the images held of the Soviet
Union. As a rule, the more fervent the desire for peace at any price and the
more vivid the visions of the nuclear holocaust and its imminence, the
greater the internal pressure has been to redefine the nature of the Soviet
system and discount criticisms directed against it. Insofar as the totalitarian
image of the Soviet Union invited strong criticism and stressed the uniquely
repressive characteristics of such societies, it had to be jettisoned—at first
by experts, and then by the media and by the educated general public.

A 1984 survey by Daniel Yankelovitch and John Dole illustrates the relationship between the fear of nuclear war and the changing conceptions of
the Soviet Union and what attitudes toward it were considered appropriate.
It was found that "Americans have come to believe that nuclear war is
unwinnable, unsurvivable." Moreover, "the public now is having second
thoughts about the dangers of. . . an assertive posture at a time when the
United States is no longer seen to maintain nuclear superiority."

The Vietnam defeat made a distinctive contribution to the development
of these attitudes: "From our Vietnam experience, voters draw the lesson

that we must keep uppermost in mind the limits of American power. . . . [W]e must avoid being provocative and confrontational." Clearly, there has been an upsurge of fear about nuclear war. Of those surveyed, 38 per cent believe that such a war is likely to occur within the next ten years and 50 per cent of those who believe this are under thirty. It may be noted that such fears suggest a connection between trust in deterrence on the one hand and American nuclear superiority on the other. In other words, it appears that people felt less threatened when U.S. superiority was unquestioned than when a different balance of power is established.

The Yankelovitch survey found a readiness on the part of Americans to blame their country for the poor relations with the Soviet Union: "Huge majorities (76 per cent of those surveyed) feel that America has been less forthcoming in working things out with the Russians than it might be and that we have to share some of their blame for the deterioration in the relationship." It is significant that, according to the findings of this survey, younger and better educated Americans are more willing to give the benefit of doubt to the Soviet regime and indicate more trusting attitudes: "[T]hey are almost totally free of the ideological hostility that the majority of Americans feel toward the Soviet Union." Even more significantly, these younger Americans are more skeptical in some ways of their own authorities than of those of the Soviet Union: "[Y]oung Americans. . .believe the degree of Soviet cheating is overstated by those who oppose negotiating with them." Fifty-nine per cent of those under thirty expressed this view.

While most respondents expressed great fear of nuclear war, the Soviet Union itself was seen as less threatening, a country not interested in expanding its influence or imposing its social-political systems on others. Thus "by a margin of 67 per cent to 28 per cent, people agree that we should let the Communists have their system while we have ours, that 'there is room in the world for both.'" Likewise, "by a margin of 59 per cent to 19 per cent, Americans also say we would be better off if we stopped treating the Soviets as enemies and tried to hammer out our differences in a live-and-let-live spirit." Evidently, neither survey designers nor respondents gave much thought to the possibility that the Soviet Union may be deeply committed to a hostile view of the United States and that such an attitude has deep ideological and political roots.

PEACE AND FEAR

What exactly is the connection between the peace movements and the fear of nuclear war? The most plausible answer is that these movements emerge in response to such fears and reflect them. At the same time, the peace and anti-nuclear movements themselves stimulate such fears by constantly dwelling on the horrors of nuclear destruction and their likelihood unless the policies they advocate are introduced. Much of what goes under "peace studies" in schools and colleges consists of the vividly detailed depiction of the gruesome consequences of nuclear war.

If, as suggested earlier, the peace and anti-nuclear movements have become a major influence on perceptions of the Soviet Union in the 1980s — and a major source of reinvigorated misconceptions of it — it is important to understand the characteristics and origins of these movements and the broader cultural and political context in which they function. The most immediate cause for their resurgence appears to be the installation of intermediate-range missiles by NATO in Western Europe, a measure which stimulated a vigorous Soviet effort to thwart such action by diplomatic, political, and propaganda campaigns. While the Soviet Union sought to stimulate and infiltrate Western peace movements in order to achieve such specific goals, these activities were probably also conditioned by a changed vision of the West, and especially the United States, in the post-Vietnam era. In the words of Feher and Heller, Hungarian émigré scholars:

> They [Soviet leaders] are more and more convinced especially after Vietnam and the Watergate affair (which for them was the ultimate proof of the contemptible lack of authority in this unruly society), that the West has very weak knees and that a combination of menacing gestures and peace-loving phrases will force Western countries into important political and economic concessions.[18]

It is of interest to note that Western susceptibilities to apocalyptic fears have deep roots and preceded the invention of nuclear weapons. Today, it is largely forgotten that, as Malcolm Muggeridge recalls, similar sentiments were widespread before the outbreak of World War II:

> We had all been talking about war, for, literally, years past. It would be the end of civilization. . . .Our cities would be razed to the ground in the twinkling of the eye. . . .There is no defense against aerial bombardment. Many thus held forth with great vigour and authority at dinner tables, in clubs and railway carriages; as did leading articles, sermons. . .after-dinner speeches at gatherings like the League of Nations Union and the Peace Pledge Union. . . .Books appeared interminably on

the subject with lurid blurbs. . . . Films were made about it, garden fêtes dedicated to it, tiny tots lisped rhymes about it. All agreed that another war was unthinkable, unspeakable, inconceivable and must at all costs be averted.[19]

THE DOOMSDAY ATMOSPHERE

Such a sense of impending doom before World War II followed closely upon the heels of the Depression and the economic crisis and social dislocations it produced; it was a time conducive to a vision of the West as decadent and worthy of being judged severely—perhaps of being destroyed. Similarly unflattering images of the West, and especially of the United States, are rife today: heedlessly immersed in an irrational and lethal arms race, misusing its science and technology, polluting its environment, appropriating the resources of the world for purposes of frivolous consumption, exploiting the Third World, becoming increasingly impersonal, bureaucratized, and dehumanized—it is hardly surprising if such images inspire (or reflect) loathing and the attendant anticipation of impending, well-deserved punishment. As Feher and Heller put it, "The Doomsday atmosphere. . .has to be understood in a literal sense. . . .The ultimate content of this anxiety is the emphatic feeling of a New Fall. . .the conviction that 'progress' was poison."[20]

ENHANCING TRUST

As if to counteract these terrifying visions, which the peace movement itself has helped to stimulate and perpetuate, ideologues and activists have begun to emphasize the unity of mankind, the humanity and basic goodness of ordinary people, and, more specifically, the redeeming results of grass-roots contacts between American and Soviet citizens. Activities enhancing understanding and trust are encouraged—peace cruises and peace treks, jointly climbing mountains, riding bicycles, singing folk songs, attending storytellers' conferences, playing volleyball, eating hamburgers, exchanging photos of children, women sharing special concerns about peace and war. Such attitudes were not limited to peace activists. Charles Wick, head of the U.S. Information Agency said: "The exciting thing about this [exchange] agreement is that it will promote the kind of understanding and mutual trust. . .on which can be built a genuine foundation for genuine arms control. When people understand each other, governments cannot be far behind."[21]

In fact a curious duality permeates the peace movement, a readiness to oscillate between profound gloom and childlike optimism. On the one hand, the imminence of nuclear holocaust is endlessly reiterated, and its horrors are conjured up in the darkest colors. On the other hand, it is constantly stressed that the conflict between the superpowers has, in effect, no objective basis but is a product of irrational, mutually reinforcing fears, misunderstandings, misperceptions, stereotypes, and mistrust, that can be dispelled only by personal warmth and an abundance of contacts and meetings by the citizens of the two countries. It follows that views critical of the Soviet Union harm the cause of peace and impede mutual understanding because they engender or reinforce mistrust and suspicion that in turn fuel the arms race. The similarities, not the differences, are emphasized: "People who cultivate wheat can't possibly want war." A member of an American women's delegation seeking dialogue wrote: "What we lacked in knowledge we made up for in enthusiasm, and we shared a sort of innocent faith that the women of our two countries were probably more alike than different."[22]

The proposition that a major source of tension between the two countries has been due to misperceptions and misunderstandings has also been adopted by such specialists on Soviet affairs as Marshall Shulman of Columbia University (formerly of the State Department). He wrote: "The hostility did not grow out of any natural antipathy between the peoples of the two countries but with the passage of time each has come to be so persuaded of the malign intent of the other that it has become difficult to distinguish what is real and what is fancied in the perceptions each holds of the other."[23] Richard Barnet, author of *The Giants*, argued that "the cold war is a history of mutually reinforcing misconceptions" and that "monumental misunderstandings" occurred in Soviet-American relations.[24]

Peace activists took it upon themselves to dispel such misconceptions and prevent the rise of new ones. A much-favored method, which became highly popular in the 1980s, has been the establishment of ties between American and Soviet communities in the framework of the sister-city program. The latter firmly embraced, in effect institutionalized, the major American misconceptions and illusions about Soviet society and especially its political institutions.

In my own town—Northampton, Massachusetts—prompted by a vocal group of peace-loving citizens, the mayor addressed the following letter to his presumed counterpart, the mayor of the Soviet town of Yelabuga, which was selected for Northampton by the Ground Zero Pairing Project, a national organization promoting sister cities:

> Your city of Yelabuga of the USSR and our city of Northampton, Mass., USA, have much in common. We are about the same size and we are located in an attractive area. More importantly, we are united in our love for our children and hopes for their future.[25]

While the goodwill underlying these sentiments is not in doubt, the attribution of meaningful commonality borders on the surrealistic. To be sure, the mayor could have added that we are also united with the citizens of Yelabuga (and of other Soviet cities, or for that matter non-Soviet cities and citizens!) in preferring pleasure to pain, health to sickness, a good diet to a poor one, fresh to polluted air, and making love rather than war.

At the town meeting devoted to discussing the establishment of sister-city ties, much was said about the importance of communications between Americans and the Soviet people. But what exactly should or could be communicated? Several speakers suggested with commendable candor that the communications on our part should be "completely innocuous" and non-political. "Praise them"; "Forget about advertising ourselves"; "They should find out that we are people too." In other words, highlight the similarities; play down the differences.

Yet it is the differences that matter most, especially in the context peace activists are most concerned with — namely, the citizens' access to government and their influence on its policies. For example, if Soviet citizens have any idea about the magnitude of Soviet military expenditures and believe that the money could be better spent on human welfare, they refrain from revealing such sentiments; if they are unhappy with Soviet intervention in Afghanistan, they don't make their feelings publicly known. If they are not unhappy, that, too, reveals a profound asymmetry between their attitude and those of many Americans vocally opposed to any American military intervention abroad.

If they had a better understanding of the nature of the Soviet system, peace activists would realize that there is no such thing, as far as Soviet citizens are concerned, as spontaneous, informal, and risk-free protest against official policies, or a similar, unauthorized, grass-roots contact with groups of Americans free of governmental supervision and manipulation. From its earliest beginnings, the Soviet authorities abhorred this or any other kind of spontaneity in political life and have done everything in their power—which is considerable—to extinguish such initiatives. Only by wishfully projecting upon the Soviet system characteristics it does not have can American peace activists believe that they will do business with their Soviet "counterparts." Worst of all, the vast majority of Soviet citizens do not even believe that they should be in a position to influence government policy.

Such misunderstandings may help to explain why only twenty-six Soviet towns responded to the invitation of one thousand American towns to join hands in the pursuit of peace and why, in at least one instance, an American town (Greenbelt, Maryland) was "paired" with a Soviet "counterpart" that boasted a forced labor camp and KGB prison.

At the confluence of the peace movement and the adversary culture, a new set of factors comes into play that contributes to the misconceptions of the Soviet Union.

HOSTILITY TOWARD THE UNITED STATES

While peace activists generally refrain from criticism of the Soviet Union, they are inclined to criticize the United States—its foreign policy, domestic institutions, prevailing values, and policies. It is hard to know whether or not those attracted to the peace movements are predisposed, to begin with, toward a highly critical view of American society, or if such attitudes develop in the course of involvement with such groups, subcultures, and their associated activities. Whatever the reason—and I am inclined to believe that it is the former—there is a striking contrast between the willingness to give the benefit of doubt to Soviet policies and the readiness to hold the American government responsible for a wide range of global problems, including the arms race and Soviet-American tensions. Following the Chernobyl disaster, two American peace activists sent a letter to the *New York Times* that offered a benign interpretation of the withholding of information by the Soviets and excused it on the grounds of an apparently laudable "tendency on the part of the Soviet leadership to downplay catastrophes and instead offer reassurance to the Soviet people so as to prevent emotional distress." They also argued that such withholding of information ("this practice of governmental and media protection") was beneficial for mental health and made Soviet youth more optimistic about world peace.[26] It is not hard to imagine their response if the American authorities had attempted to conceal—in the interests of public emotional welfare and mental health—a malfunction of an American nuclear power plant.

Peace activists and social critics alike tend to find the source of Soviet-American rivalry and conflict (and a host of other problems) in the nature of American society. Ramsey Clark, for instance, has argued that "We need a revolutionary change in values, because we glorify violence and want 'things' inordinately. . . . Money dominates politics in America and, through politics, government." He also favored unilateral disarmament on the part of the United States. A professor of "medical-psychiatric anthropology" argued on the op-ed page of the *New York Times* that the United States has become so militaristic that even the music played on classical-music radio stations was "intended to rouse a martial spirit." Not only music but also "cinema [and] fashion all express that toughness, defiance, eagerness for unbridled action, [and] truculence that lie at the heart of the. . . 'national mood.' They are part of a great national preparation—for war."[27] A book-length study was dedicated to the proposition that belief in a Soviet threat (in an "illusory enemy") was nothing but a product of the American domestic political process and of the groups dominating it.

Such views have been widespread in the 1980s and associated with cross-fertilization between the anti-nuclear peace movement and the survival of the adversary culture—that is to say, elements and activists of the protest movements of the 1960s. It was not surprising that "the nuclear disarmament rally. . .expected to draw hundreds of thousands of people into Manhattan. . .has been conceived and organized by groups with a history of protest reaching back to anti-Vietnam War days and by a new set of protesters."

Vaclav Havel, a Czech dissident, captured the roots of the connection between the Western peace movements and a broader agenda of protest and aspiration:

> For them the fight for peace is probably something more than simply a matter of certain demands for disarmament. . .an opportunity to build unconforming, uncorrupted social structures, an opportunity for life in a humanly richer community, for self-realization outside the stereotypes of a consumer society, and for expressing their resistance to those stereotypes.[28]

Although the self-critical sentiments that foster the more favorable or benefit-of-doubt attitudes toward the Soviet Union are predominantly produced by conditions within American society, there have also been

Soviet contributions to these attitudes. In particular, expressions of hostility and guilt-inducing techniques have been widely used—for example, accusations of American warmongering combined with constant reminders of the number of Soviet people killed in World War II, far exceeding the number of Americans killed, a reminder apt to make most Americans feel guilty and at the same time impress them with the sincerity of the Soviet desire for peace. Expressions of hostility by themselves can lead to a characteristic, good-natured American soul-searching that ultimately yields the conclusion that amends must be made and critical judgments of the Soviet Union revised. Richard Pipes observed that "a strong residue of Protestant ethic causes Americans to regard all hostility to them as being at least in some measure brought about by their own faults. . . . It is quite possible to exploit this tendency. . . .Thus is created an atmosphere conducive to concessions whose purpose is to propitiate the allegedly injured party."[29]

MORAL EQUIVALENCE

Many of the trends and tendencies associated with the misconceptions of the Soviet system discussed above have found support and new expression in the currently popular moral-equivalence thesis first brought into critical focus by Jeane Kirkpatrick. The core of the idea is that there are no important differences between the United States and the Soviet Union—usually referred to as the superpowers—and certainly none that would give any moral credit to the United States over the USSR.

The moral-equivalence thesis allows those embracing it to appear both objective and detached (they don't favor either of the rival superpowers) and at the same time provides a respectable retreat for those who had earlier sympathized with the Soviet Union, which is now seen as neither better nor worse than the United States. Most importantly, by obliterating important distinctions between the two societies it allows for more effective denigration of the United States.

In fact, contrary to appearances, the moral-equivalence school is far from being truly neutral or objective but usually harbors some degree of hostility toward the United States. Those who subscribe to it tend to be far more critical of the United States than of the USSR, and their critiques of the latter are perfunctory, while their critiques of the United States are intense, passionate, and specific.

The moral-equivalence thesis reflects developments noted earlier: (1) the passing of the idealization of the Soviet Union (which, however, has not necessarily been replaced by a seriously critical understanding of it); (2) the rise of the peace movement and the pressures it has exerted against critical views of the Soviet Union; (3) the survival and institutionalization of the adversary culture that does not take kindly to regarding the United States as better than any other country, and especially one that continues to claim socialist credentials; and (4) the moral-equivalence position also appeals to those anti-anti-Communist intellectuals and opinion makers who remain apprehensive about the possibility that a strongly critical stand toward the Soviet Union might put them in the unsavory company of cold warriors and right-wingers.

A social-scientific precursor of the moral-equivalence school may be found in the convergence theory that was fashionable in the 1960s and postulated growing similarities between the United States and the Soviet Union due to the imperatives of modernization. This, however, was an essentially optimistic view: The Soviet Union was to become more liberal and democratic, gradually adopting the practices and values of advanced pluralistic societies (such as the United States). The message of moral equivalence is more cynical, stressing the unappealing attributes that both societies have in common—a state of affairs that should discourage the United States and its champions from assuming an air of moral superiority.

Thus Richard Barnet points out—in what might be regarded as a definitive handbook on moral equivalence, *The Giants*—that "the CIA and the KGB have the same conspiratorial world view," that "in both countries leading military bureaucrats constitute a potent political force," and "the military establishments in the United States and the Soviet Union are. . .each other's best allies," that "Khrushchev and Dulles were perfect partners," that "both sides have a professional interest in the nostalgic illusion of victory through secret weapons," that "both societies were suffering a crisis of legitimacy," that "both are preoccupied with security problems," that "military bureaucracies are developing in the Soviet Union that are mirror images of American bureaucracies," that "the madness of one bureaucracy sustains the other," and that "each [country] is a prisoner of a sixty-year-old obsession."

The affinity toward the moral-equivalence thesis also feeds on a generally diminished capacity to make distinctions that has been with us since the 1960s, a legacy of the anti-intellectualism of that period. Other examples of this attitude include the propensity to dilute distinctions between mental health and mental illness, religion and therapy, learning and entertainment, political freedom and repression, art and politics, and what is private and what is public.

Thus in the final analysis we are led back to the suggestion that conditions within the United States are the most important determinants of American perceptions of the Soviet Union. It is unfortunate that these conditions, more often than not, predispose to misconceptions rather than to understanding.

FOOTNOTES

1. Claude Cockburn, *Crossing the Line* (London: McGibbon and Kee, 1958) p. 123.

2. William Barrett, *The Truants—Adventures Among Intellectuals* (New York: Anchor/ Doubleday, 1982) p. 247.

3. Joseph Finder, *Red Carpet* (New York: Holt, Reinhart, and Winston, 1983) p. 316.

4. Donald M. Kendall, "Give Moscow 'Carrots,'" *The New York Times*, February 9, 1983.

5. Vladimir Bukovsky, "Mesmerized by the Bear," *The Washington Times*, May 27, 1986.

6. George F. Kennan, "Historian Says Soviets are Like Americans," *Daily Hampshire Gazette*, November 19, 1983.

7. George F. Kennan, *The Nuclear Delusion—Soviet-American Relations in the Atomic Age* (New York: Pantheon, 1982) pp. 64, 65.

8. Jerry F. Hough, "Why the Russians Invaded," *The Nation*, March 1, 1980.

9. Theodore Von Laue, "Stalin Among the Moral and Political Imperatives, or How to Judge Stalin?" *The Soviet Union* (Part 1).

10. Irving Kristol, "Foreign Policy in an Age of Ideology," *The National Interest*, Fall, 1985, p. 11.

11. E. J. Epstein, "The Andropov File," *The New Republic*, February 7, 1983.

12. Hedrick Smith, "Impressions of M. Gorbachev," *The New York Times*, September 12, 1985.

13. Paul Hollander, *Soviet and American Society: A Comparison* (New York: Oxford University Press, 1973) p. 110.

14. D. E. Powell, "In Pursuit of Interest Groups in the USSR," *The Soviet Union* (Part 1).

15. J. Hough and M. Fainsod, *How the Soviet Union is Governed* (Cambridge: Harvard University Press, 1979) pp. 297-98.

16. Peter Kenez, "Stalinism as Humdrum Politics," *Russian Review*, 1986 (forthcoming) pp. 4-5.

17. *Ibid.* pp. 8-9.

18. F. Feher and A. Heller, "On Being Anti-Nuclear in Soviet Societies," *Telos*, Fall, 1983, p. 148.

19. Malcolm Muggeridge, *Chronicles of Wasted Time: The Infernal Grove* (New York: William Morrow, 1974) p. 73.

20. Feher and Heller, *op. cit.* p. 161.

21. P. Samuel, "Mr. Wick Goes to Moscow," *The National Interest*, Spring, 1986, pp. 102-3.

22. J. Howard, "American and Soviet Women—Are we Really so Different?" *New*

Woman, April, 1986, p. 122; and A. Russell, "Reaching Beyond Politics," *Foundation News*, November–December 1983, p. 41.

23. Marshall Shulman, "What the Russians Really Want," *Harpers*, April 1984, p. 63.

24. Richard Barnet, *The Giants—Russia and America* (New York: Simon and Schuster, 1977) pp. 95, 14.

25. Paul Hollander, "What Northampton and Yelabuga Have in Common?" *Daily Hampshire Gazette*, January 16, 1984.

26. E. Chivian and J. E. Mack, "Soviet Minds Sheltered From Catastrophes," (Letter) *The New York Times*, May 15, 1986.

27. H. F. Stein, "Dum. Dum. Dum. Dum. Dum." *The New York Times*, September 22, 1980.

28. V. Havel, "Peace: The View From Prague," *New York Review of Books*, November 21, 1985.

29. Richard Pipes, "Some Organizational Principles of Soviet Foreign Policy." Memorandum for the Subcommittee on National Security of the U.S. Senate, Washington, D. C., 1972, p. 14.

Select Bibliography

"America's Peace Movement, 1900–1986," including essays by Ralph D. Nurnberger, Robert Woito, and George Weigel, in *The Wilson Quarterly*, New Year's Issue, 1987.

Barron, John. "The KGB's Magical War for Peace." *Reader's Digest*, October, 1982.

_____. *The KGB Today: The Hidden Hand*. New York: Reader's Digest Press, 1983.

Bukovsky, Vladimir. "The Peace Movement and the Soviet Union." *Commentary*, May, 1982.

_____. *To Build a Castle: My Life as a Dissenter*. Viking Press, 1979.

_____. *The Peace Movement and the Soviet Union*. Orwell Press, 1982.

Chalfont, Lord Alun. "The Great Unilateralist Illusion." *Encounter*, April 1983.

English, Raymond (ed.) *Ethics and Nuclear Arms*. Washington, D.C.: Ethics and Public Policy Center, 1985. See especially the essay by Frans A. M. Alting von Geusau on "Nuclear Pacifism and True Peace."

Godson, Roy, Vladimir Bukovsky, and Paul Anastasi. *Soviet Active Measures, People-to-People Contacts, and the Helsinki Process*. Washington, D.C.: National Strategy Information Center Monograph, 1986.

_____. and William Schultz. *Diesinformatzia: The Strategy of Soviet Information*. New York: Berkeley Press, 1986.

_____. (ed.) *Disinformation: Soviet Active Measures and Disinformation Forecast*. A Quarterly journal published by Regnery Gateway in Washington, D.C.

Hakovirta, Harto. "The Soviet Union and the Varieties of Neutrality in Western Europe." *World Politics*, July, 1983.

Hoffer, Eric. *The True Believer*. New York: Harper and Row, 1951.

Hollander, Paul. *Soviet and American Society: A Comparison*. Oxford University Press, 1973.

_____. *Political Pilgrims: Travels of Western Intellectuals to the Soviet Union, China, and Cuba, 1928–78*. Oxford University Press, 1981.

Hook, Sidney. *Marx and the Marxists: An Ambiguous Legacy*. Van Nos Reinhold, 1955.

_____. *Revolutionary Reform and Social Justice: Studies in the Theory and Practice of Marxism*. New York University Press, 1975.

Joshua, Wynfred. "Soviet Manipulation of the European Peace Movement." *Strategic Review*, Winter, 1983.

Krushchev, Nikita. *Krushchev's Mein Kampf*. New York: Belmont Books, 1961.

Koestler, Arthur. *Darkness at Noon*. London: D. Hardy, 1940.

_____, and Richard H. Crossman (eds.) *The God That Failed*. Arno, 1982; reprint of original 1949 edition.

Lefever, Ernest W., and E. Stephen Hunt (eds.) *The Apocalyptic Premise: Nuclear Arms Debated*. Washington, D.C.: Ethics and Public Policy Center, 1982. See especially Part Two, "The Peace Movement."

Mercer, Paul. *Peace of the Dead*. London: Policy Research Publications Ltd., 1986.

Orwell, George. *Nineteen Eighty-Four*. New York: Harcourt, Brace, Jovanovich, 1963.

Smith, Thomas B. *Educating for Disaster: The Nuclear Spectre in America's Classrooms*. Evanston, IL: UCA Books, 1986.

Solzhenitsyn, Alexandr. *The Gulag Archipelago*. 3 volumes. New York: Harper and Row, 1974.

Sowell, Thomas. *Marxism*. New York: William Morrow and Co., 1985.

Toth, Robert C. "Soviet 'Peace Drive' Keeps Its Momentum." *Los Angeles Times*, September 24, 1986.

Towle, Philip, Iain Elliot, and Gerald Frost. *Protest and Perish: A Critique of Unilateralism*. London: Institute for European Defence and Strategic Studies, 1982.

Vermaat, J. A. Emerson. "Moscow and the European Peace Movement." Ethics and Public Policy Center Reprint Series, April 1983.

_____. "The Strange Phenomenon of the 'Generals for Peace.' " *Strategic Review*, Spring, 1985

Wettig, Gerhard. "The Western Peace Movement in Moscow's Longer View." *Strategic Review*, Spring, 1984.

Index